CONVOY ESCORT COMMANDER

Vice-Admiral
Sir Peter Gretton
K.C.B., D.S.O., O.B.E., D.S.C.

SAPERE
BOOKS

CONVOY ESCORT
COMMANDER

Published by Sapere Books.

20 Windermere Drive, Leeds, England, LS17 7UZ,
United Kingdom

saperebooks.com

ISBN: 978-1-80055-263-0.

To the men of the Allied Merchant Navies and of the Allied Navies and Air Forces who gave their lives in the Battle of the Atlantic, 3rd September 1939 to 8th May 1945

TABLE OF CONTENTS

INTRODUCTION

I EMBARKED on this book, at the suggestion of friends, in 1956. Before starting work, I asked two senior Admirals who were serving at the Admiralty whether they thought that it would be correct for an officer still on the active list to publish a book about his wartime experiences. Both replied, 'Yes, it would be good for the Navy,' so I went ahead. Later on, when the book was nearly finished, I wrote to the Admiralty for permission to consult some special papers in connection with the book. The reply gave me permission to see the records, but added that it was against Admiralty policy for serving officers to publish books about their experiences. This accounts for the delay in publication!

The text has been amended a little since 1956 and some additions made too, for since then much official history has been written and several good personal accounts published which enable one to get a much more accurate picture of what really happened. In particular, Ronald Seth's excellent book *The Fiercest Battle*, which describes the passage of Convoy ONS 5 in which my group took a prominent part, gives many facts, especially about the fate of the merchant ships, which I did not know before. So I hope that this version will be better in every way than the original one.

I kept no diary during the war and few records. I have an indifferent memory for dates and for some of the more unpleasant experiences. So I apologize in advance for any mistakes, which are mine alone. Moreover, any opinions expressed are also my own and have no official sanction.

The main reason why I wrote this book was that I had a long apprenticeship in convoy work during 1939, 1940 and 1941 which proved an excellent preparation for the task of escort commander in the years 1942-4[1]. In the spring of 1943, B 7 Escort Group had the good fortune to be engaged in three successive convoy battles against wolf packs assembled in great strength. At the end of May, Doenitz withdrew his U-boats from the North Atlantic to refit and re-arm, and the first and most critical part of the battle had been won. Then, in October 1943, after a quiet summer, my group had a busy and fruitful cruise of twenty-five days at sea as a support group with a roving commission between threatened convoys. This was the time of the introduction of the German acoustic torpedo, which listened for one's propeller noises and then homed on the screws — and of the return of the U-boats to the North Atlantic.

I believe therefore that although I have no special claim to skill in sinking submarines, I am well qualified to discuss the art of escorting convoys across the North Atlantic. Moreover, many of the lessons learnt at such cost in the last war are being forgotten, just as precisely the same lessons were forgotten after 1918 and after the Napoleonic wars. I hope that this book will jog a few memories, for the facts are still important even in a nuclear age. I have confined the preaching mostly to the last two chapters. These will seem a little technical, but will I hope be found interesting. The remainder of the book describes my personal experiences.

My group was lucky to have been closely involved in two of the turning points of the Battle of the Atlantic, and doubly lucky because in each case we were allowed a few months'

---

[1] For my naval background prior to the outbreak of war, see Appendix I.

preparation of tough but uneventful escort duty, during which we were able to develop into a well-knit and competent team. If we had met the enemy in such numbers earlier, the result might well have been different.

In fact, in retrospect, it all seems miraculous. What would the Naval Staff College appreciation have been in, say, 1934 of a situation in which a convoy of forty ships with a best speed of seven knots was preparing to sail westwards in ballast in bad weather, with an escort consisting of two destroyers, one frigate, and four corvettes which were slower than the opposing U-boats? — In which air cover for the convoy was scanty generally and non existent in the mid-Ocean gap, and in which no less than sixty U-boats were deployed in the Atlantic, poised to attack the convoy at one stage or another of its passage? — A situation, also, in which the enemy were able to break our cyphers and thus establish the position of most convoys in the Atlantic? I think the staff solution would have been 'annihilation'. But the outcome of the passage of convoy ONS 5 was very different.

I realized at the time and I realize even more clearly now how lucky I was to have had such an outstanding team. The Captains of the ships, whom I have listed by name in Appendix II, were well above average. They were keen, competent and full of initiative. Their subsequent careers, in war and peace, in many parts of the world and in many professions, have been uniformly successful, and as naval officers, as master mariners, as industrialists and as chartered accountants, all have prospered. I was also blessed with a very good staff.

I have been given much help in writing this book and a list of names would be a long one. But my special thanks are due to the Admiralty Records Office and to the Historical Sections of the Admiralty and the Air Ministry.

PETER GRETTON
Wimbledon, 1st June 1963.

1. EAST COAST CONVOY

WHEN the war started in September 1939, I left the Royal Naval College, Dartmouth, where I was serving on the staff, at short notice; and after a fortnight's gunnery course to learn about the new form of armament with which I should have to compete, I was appointed First Lieutenant of the *Vega*, a World War I destroyer, which was being converted to anti-aircraft and antisubmarine (A/S) escort duties.

The start was in the best traditions. My appointment directed me to report to Portsmouth dockyard to join the ship, but after my Munich crisis experience I was too wary to be caught by that game again — I took the precaution of ringing up a friend at Pompey first, and found, as I expected, that my ship was at Devonport. (During the Munich mobilization of 1938, I had left the West Country by car to join the *Vanquisher*, which the Admiralty practical-joke department had informed me was at Weymouth; and after drawing Portland, Portsmouth, and Chatham blank, I finally ran her to earth lying at a buoy at Sheerness!)

On arrival at Devonport, I found the *Vega*'s conversion still only half finished, and a most important month was spent before commissioning. At that time, we all thought that we were going to miss the great battle. Why, I cannot think, because it must have been clear that the war was not going to be a short one. But we spent much time calling on those lucky ships which were operating at sea, and used to listen greedily to their experiences.

Eventually, after four long weeks, the time came to commission. There were only about a dozen men standing by her at the dockyard, together with most of the officers, and we were able to make our plans and be as well prepared as forethought could make possible.

The morning of commissioning was fine, and the official inspection of the ship, and the brief ceremony when the dockyard handed her over to us, went well. Directly the Captain of the Dockyard, who had done the inspection, left, however, the rain started to fall as only West Country rain can, and the commissioning proper started. The ship was manned by a Portsmouth crew whose train arrived over an hour late. The station was some way away, there were no buses, covered lorries were impossible to find, and both the men and their hammocks were wet before they were finally on board. It was pitch dark — for the blackout was taken very seriously in those days — and it is still a mystery to me how we managed to get them all, with their bags and hammocks, on board safely.

We then carried out a careful muster, since the list which had been sent on ahead bore little relation to the names of the men who had actually arrived and, after a good deal of sorting out, it was discovered that only half the stokers were present and that the telegraphists were also adrift. Frantic signals to Portsmouth produced the men next day — there had been some slip up in the drill that end, but the mistake did not help our plans!

At that time there were practically no escort vessels in commission, so it was important to get on the job as soon as possible. Our programme of commissioning and trials was most ambitious, and we were due to go out for gun trials within three days of the ship's company arriving on board. They were nightmare days. Half the sailors were R.N.V.R.s, a cheerful lot, but with singularly little experience of ships or the sea, and they had to be shown everything. We had to fill up with ammunition, provisions and stores and prepare for sea in the short time available; work was never finished before ten or eleven at night. By the skin of our teeth we managed to make the date, and early one morning in October we slipped and went down the Hamoaze, to swing compasses in Plymouth Sound and then carry out gun trials.

It was a day which will be difficult to forget. It was blowing very hard, and as soon as we had poked our nose outside the breakwater half the ship's company and all the dockyard mateys, who were aboard for the trials, were down and out. The guns were new, and each twin mounting had to be fired at several elevations, first one gun at a time then both together. We did the after mounting first with fair success, as it was comparatively dry there and the motion not too bad; but by the time we had reached the forward mounting, the ship was pitching heavily into steep seas, and only one of the gun's crew was capable of action.

I was feeling far from well myself, but pride is a great support in these circumstances and, with the help of the trials officer (a tall and hefty gunnery expert), the gunner's mate and I succeeded in loading, training, elevating and firing both guns in the mounting. Then, drenched with salt water, we were able to report that the guns were satisfactory, and the ship returned to the Sound to land the trials party.

We sailed immediately for Portland to 'work up'. The journey was not a quiet one. Our asdic operators, being new and extremely keen, discovered U-boats in every shoal of fish or wreck lying on the bottom — and our passage up the Channel was marked by a trail of depth-charge explosions, with their aftermath of dead fish floating belly upwards in the water.

But we got there without disaster, and even the Captain, who luckily was a navigating specialist with a remarkably calm temperament, must have been pleased to see the ship securely moored to a buoy. The officers were as new to the game as the sailors, and odd events would keep occurring.

The 'working up' consisted of intensive exercises in every form of warfare which we were likely to meet. We practised sinking submarines, we let off large numbers of rounds at sleeve targets towed by Fleet Air Arm planes, and we fired at surface targets, too. According to peacetime standards, it cannot be said that everything went well, but that was hardly to be expected. There were some remarkable scenes.

We had one of the first R.N.V.R. H.A. units which were raised as complete teams, designed to man one four-inch twin H.A. gun with its associated fire-control gear. The scheme was admirable, but it had little time to develop properly before the war came. Our unit, for instance, had never seen either a gun or its control gear. Some of the men were ill-cast and all the men manning the telephones seemed to lack teeth, which made them unintelligible even to fellow Merseyside men. But we changed them around, mixed up the gun's crew with the 'regular' sailors in the ship and we soon had an excellent team.

The gun crews were gun shy, and long delays spoilt the shoots; our boat work was dreadful; I was never happy except when the motor-boat was safely hoisted inboard, and the whaler's crew seemed incapable of pulling an oar. We would take hours to secure to a buoy, afterwards finding great difficulty in unshackling the cable again; and the 'buoy-jumper', a heroic individual blessed with no imagination, had more than one cold swim as a result of his efforts to sit a bucking buoy. Winter at Portland is not the ideal time to work up a ship.

My worst moment was, I think, one morning when we were about to shift berth to an oiler. After a long and blasphemous hour on the foc'sle trying to unshackle the cable from the buoy in a nasty chop, I was able to report 'Ready to slip' to the Captain. As the slip wire was let go and the ship went ahead, I glanced down the side to see if all was ready to go alongside. To my horror I saw the motor-boat, still secured to the lower boom by a long boat-rope, being towed through the water at high speed. She had no one on board, and was filling up with water rapidly. The Captain stopped the ship just in time, and there was a long and irritating delay before we were able to clear the side for going to the oiler. The messenger who had been sent to ask one of the officers to get the boat away before slipping had delivered such a garbled message that nothing had been done, and those on the upper deck who noticed her in this dangerous situation were so bone-headed that they said nothing about it.

We worked very hard, much to the disgust of some of the new hands from the Mersey who still retained strong trade union ideas about working all Sunday, as well as every other day of the week.

In time, thanks to the imperturbability of the Captain, things went a little more smoothly; and we sailed for our base, Rosyth, joining the escort of an east-coast convoy en route. In these days of radar, of expert coders trained to deal with the wireless traffic, and of war-experienced officers and men, it is difficult to remember the difficulties of those first months. We wasted much time and ammunition trying to sink floating mines which had broken adrift from their fields — eventually, I found a really good rifle-shot and we spent less time at the game — we were constantly going to action stations before investigating ships sighted in the darkness; the Gunner and I were the only officers with watch-keeping tickets, and there were always large numbers of cyphers to be flogged out when we were not on watch. Wren cypher staffs ashore were not then so good as they were later, and some messages had many mistakes, all of which had to be puzzled out.

I think that most of the lessons learnt have been remembered. Shore headquarters are now fully manned in many peacetime exercises, and we should avoid these mistakes in future, but it is as well to set them down now. Nothing can replace realism in peacetime exercises, and the worse the weather the better the value, for only then is it established that the equipment will stand the strain of war. It does the officers and men no harm either!

The merchant ships were not accustomed to keeping station, did not like convoys, and took every opportunity to slip away from them, usually with disastrous results to the culprit, so that the four-day passage to our base was a good deal more tiring than we had expected.

Five months passed quickly on the east-coast route. The ship had a number of adventures, none of them very important, but they then assumed larger proportions than they do now. At first there were a few U-boats about near the coast, but air cover of convoys, the mine barrage, and one or two sinkings, discouraged them; they soon disappeared and to our disappointment we never met one. Aircraft and mines were the chief danger, with the hazards of fog and 'marine disaster', as the text books call it, coming a close third (fortunately E-boats had not then appeared on the scene). The swept channel through the enemy minefields was not so well marked as it was to be later on, the Germans had attacked several lightships, which were out of action as a result, and it was not easy to navigate these long convoys through the narrow and tricky channel.

Coastal convoys were a very different affair from ocean convoys. They were smaller for one thing and were in never more than two columns so that the ships could keep in the narrow swept channel. Their shape was long and thin, therefore, and station-keeping was even more difficult than in the open sea because of the tides and the bends in the narrow channels which twisted their way through the sand banks of the east-coast route. We used to pick up a north-bound convoy off Southend and drop it at Methyl, opposite Leith in the Firth of Forth, reversing the process shortly after arrival, and returning to Southend with a south-bound convoy.

Escorts were very few, and the difficulties can well be shown by an episode in which we were involved. We were bringing up the rear of one long convoy which stretched for several miles, in visibility which, though not foggy, was decidedly poor. The passage passed comparatively quietly, and we saw or heard no incidents of any kind. The report of proceedings was easily made out, being blank; and it was only when we arrived alongside the jetty at Rosyth that we learnt that a ship in the middle of our convoy had been mined, sunk, and had had all her crew picked up by the next ship, without ourselves or the other escort at the head of the line knowing anything about the disaster.

Mines were a menace. The magnetic mines were being used for the first time, and mixed with a quantity of the normal moored variety, were strewn liberally about our route. On one occasion, a moored minefield was discovered off Cromer just before we were due to pass through it in thick fog. The convoy was anchored hurriedly — not an easy nor a safe proceeding in low visibility — and then awaited the arrival of the clearing force of sweepers. They did not take long to come out from Hull, and started operations as soon as the fog lifted. It had been an anxious time waiting, but there was worse to come.

The sweepers, all four of them last-war coal-burners of the Pangbourne class, formed up in close quarter line, and the convoy, in single file with our ship in the van, followed at a respectful distance. There was not long to wait for the first mine to be cut. It exploded in the outer sweep of the leading ship, sending a column of water in the air and bringing the remainder of our ship's company up on deck at high speed. After that they popped up like corks, one after the other; some exploding and some floating ominously past, to give the machine-gunners and rifle-shots some excellent practice before they were sunk. We saw over a dozen mines swept up in under half an hour, all dead in the convoy's track, and we then passed thankfully on, leaving the sweepers to continue their dangerous trade. They were kept very busy indeed in those early days, and their work was not enviable.

In another fog, in the same part of the world, we had a slight collision which put us in dock for eight days. Again the convoy had been anchored, and after a long wait the fog had lifted a little. As we went ahead to regain station, a green bow-light came rushing out of the mist on our port bow. The Captain went full speed astern; but it was just too late and we hit a small tramp on the bulwarks around her starboard quarter. Her damage was negligible, but we had a nasty gash in the bows, which had been twisted and torn, fortunately above the water line. A collision mat was placed over the hole and we had no trouble in getting back to harbour.

This crash sent us into the Caledon yard at Dundee, where the opportunity was taken to fit us with degaussing gear for protection against magnetic mines. The men there worked harder than I was ever to see them work. The weather was appallingly cold during that first wartime January, but nothing seemed to stop them, and for the only time during the war our repairs were finished before time. It was a pleasure to be in such a yard and to meet managers who 'turned to with the hands' in the morning, and really knew the men and their problems.

In war, the great increase in repair work for naval ships resulted in more work going to the private ship-builder who in peace was only allowed contracts for new ships — for the Royal Dockyards then undertook all repair work. As a result knowledge of naval work was confined to a few big firms, and this had grave consequences in war. Since the war, I should add, the policy has been changed and many yards in the country now have some share in naval work.

After this incident, the regular round continued. We were spending a great deal of time at sea, but the trips never took more than three or four days, and we were reasonably sure of a 'night in' at the end of each one. Our convoys were never seriously attacked by aircraft, although a few single planes flew over once or twice and casually dropped bombs. Far the worst times were those which involved the domestic details of convoy work. Keeping up to time; arranging for ships to break away and join off the ports on the route; seeing that the rear of the long line kept in the swept channel, not at all an easy job with strong tides; and avoiding collisions in bad weather.

We had only one more excitement of any note before I left the ship. One afternoon we had just completed a north-bound passage and, after seeing most of the convoy safely anchored at Methyl, had gone on at good speed to get back to our base at Rosyth. We were due to clean boilers, and I was looking forward to a week-end with friends in Edinburgh. I went below to change into respectable clothes. No sooner had this been completed than a messenger came down to say, 'First Lieutenant required on the bridge.' One of our late convoy, which had gone on ahead towards Leith, had been blown up by a magnetic mine. Although carefully warned of the position of the German minefield, she had chosen to ignore the warning, with this inevitable result.

When we got up to her, her boats were some way off, pulling hard for Leith, but the ship was still afloat in calm water, well down by the stern. The Captain decided to try to beach her, so the whaler was lowered and we pulled across. Boarding was simple, as a ladder was hanging over the side between the dangling boats' falls; and we were soon aboard, leaving one boatkeeper in the whaler.

We went straight up on to the foc'sle head and caught a line from the ship which was lying close. Next came a grass hawser, and then a steel wire. It was heart-breaking and back-breaking work. There were only seven of us to haul in this heavy towrope; and steam had been allowed to blow off, so that the winch was useless. After tremendous efforts we succeeded in getting the end of the wire inboard; to be rewarded by a loud rending sound from aft, followed by shouts from the ship, 'Get off her quick, she's going.'

The bulk-heads aft had given way, and the stern was slowly but surely sinking below the water, while, to our discomfiture, the bows rose higher and higher. There was nothing to do but jump for it, because the deep well-deck made the climb down to a lower level a lengthy one. It was a horrible moment. The longer we waited, the higher we became. I felt like the man in the song, who stood on the burning house, while his friends shouted, 'Jump, you blighter, jump, we have a blanket here'; for by now there were many encouraging cries coming from the ship. Eventually, one brave man was persuaded to lead, and we all quickly followed him into the water. I have always hated diving, even from the lowest height, and was terrified by the prospect of jumping from this enormous altitude. But the jump was not so bad as I had expected, and, indeed, I came off best because in order to haul better on the wire I had discarded my life jacket and had had no time to put it on again. The others omitted to grasp the top of their cork jackets, and were all given a sharp blow under the chin as they hit the icy water, one man being knocked right out. After much bad language, we reached the whaler, which was being extremely clumsily handled by its single occupant, and the last we saw of the ship was a single mast surrounded by scores of the large beer barrels which had formed most of her deck cargo.

It was particularly irritating to find afterwards that our jumps had been unnecessary. However, one did acquire the experience of a genuine sinking, and I remember swimming away hard from the bow which was going down fast alongside me, for I had read much of the suction and other dangers. But I noticed nothing of it and determined then and there never to leave a ship again. It would leave me next time and I would float off!

Not long after this episode, I left the ship suddenly, just in time for the spring campaign in Norway — missing, however, the blocking of several Channel ports in which the *Vega* played a prominent and exciting part during the invasion of France and the Low Countries by the Germans.

2. NORWAY AND NARVIK

EARLY in April 1940 I was given a 'pierhead jump', as a sudden and unexpected appointment is called, to the *Cossack*, a Tribal destroyer, a flotilla of which had returned home from the Mediterranean at the beginning of the war. I joined on a Friday afternoon at Rosyth after a fearful rush, and started to find out as much as possible about my new ship without delay. I was to be a First Lieutenant again, but I was delighted as the ship was new, much bigger and belonged to the Fleet.

It was obvious that something was in the air. All shore leave had been stopped and — a fact which sent the mess decks into a buzz of rumours — not even the postman or the wardroom messman were allowed to leave the ship. Whatever was on must be important; and we searched the papers for clues and switched on the loud-speaker to listen to the B.B.C.

Captain D (Destroyers) 4's staff hurried from ship to ship looking extremely important and rather serious; and the tension grew. It seemed that there might be a battle, and I thought it might be a good plan to get the local priest down, so I sent a chit to the rest of the flotilla giving them the news. The result was astonishing — the flat outside my cabin was full of sailors throughout the dog watches. It is comforting to look back on that evening now, as the ship in the next pen was the *Ghurka*, a West Country ship who sent over a large team of cheery Irish Catholics to see the priest. There were few survivors when she was bombed and sunk only three days later.

After Divisions and Church next day, all ships of the flotilla marched their ships' companies to the jetty where the leader lay alongside; and Captain D 4 gave us a short talk. His formidable eyebrows and penetrating blue eyes were accustomed to drawing close attention from his audiences in normal times; that day, there was not a trace of the usually inevitable tooth suck from the rear of a crowd of sailors, reluctantly parted from their favourite overalls, dressed up in their best suits and made to shamble around in fours in a poor imitation of soldiers. He did not give much away except to say that he expected us all to maintain the flotilla's record; but it was enough to set us thinking hard again, for by then we all had the buzz 'Norway' and soldiers were to be seen climbing aboard some cruisers alongside the jetty.

There was an epidemic of Will-making before dinner. After dark that night, 7th April, we sailed, together with the 1st and 2nd Cruiser Squadrons and several destroyers.

The next eight days were the most crowded of my life. After one or two trips as escort to the Norwegian trade convoys, the flotilla's station-keeping was a little off-colour. Station-keeping without lights in low visibility is no rest cure at the best of times. We were the last ship but one in the line, spending the night 'concertina-ing' up and down the line, but, with the help of the Captain, who had been on the bridge all the time, we were in station by dawn.

That day was quiet, except for the 'galley buzzes', which grew and multiplied. For once we were not on the screen spread ahead of the big ships, but were working as a flotilla in close order. Early next morning the fun started. I had kept the middle watch, and had not been turned in very long when a messenger came down to say that the Captain wanted to see me on the bridge. I nipped up quickly, having only to throw off the rug under which I lay fully dressed, and heard that the *Kashmir* had been rammed by the *Kelvin*, two ships ahead of us in the line. As junior ship, we were to stand by the *Kashmir*, and the *Zulu* would act as screen for the three of us. We were furious because we thought we would miss the fun to come, but it turned out to be a blessing in disguise — owing to this affair we caught up the Narvik battle.

While on the subject of collisions, I might recall the incident which took place between two ships of one flotilla not long before. It so happened that after a recent series of mishaps involving torpedoes, mines and collisions, the *Nonsuch* was in a high state of alertness and preparedness for battle. As is the custom in all ships, the wireless operator on watch had, hung before his eyes, a board on which were pasted the current code groups for such happenings as 'Have been struck by a bomb', 'Have been torpedoed', 'Have been in collision', 'Have taken the ground', or 'Have been struck by a mine'; this was in order that no delay should occur in reporting such unfortunate events. One night the rating on watch in the *Nonsuch* wireless office heard a thump of great magnitude somewhere aft, and, with what he thought commendable promptitude, selected the last of these 'Distress groups', hurling it off into the ether, from whence it was received by the operator of the ship which had in fact been in collision with *Nonsuch*. '*Nonsuch* reports she has been hit by a mine,' the operator shouted up the voice pipe to the Captain, who instantly replied, 'Make by W/T: NOT MINE, ME.'

We closed the two ships which were in trouble, and, after a furious interchange of signals, the situation grew gradually clearer. By the time light came it had been decided that we should tow the *Kashmir*, which could make good up to ten knots but which could not steer, that the *Kelvin*, which had a very shaky bow, should steam stern first in company, and that the *Zulu* screened us ahead. The Doctor's cabin in the *Kashmir* had taken the blow, and no trace of him was ever found, but there were no other casualties.

Luckily the weather was good and it did not take long to get the tow passed, as the Captain placed us in position very neatly. Despite my lack of knowledge of the ship and its men, there were no 'hang ups'; the petty officers knew their job, and I was blessed with a torpedo gunner who had been in the ship since the commissioning and was a born seaman. Once it looked as if the formidable mass of ropes was going to jam in the fair lead; but 'Guns' was there with a handspike, and for the first but by no means last time he saved me from an unpleasant situation.

We were not seriously interrupted either, as the only outside onlooker was a seaplane which circled round for some time out of range and then flew off. We decided for our own peace of mind that it was Norwegian — there was nothing we could do about it even if it had been enemy. At length, the *Kashmir* hoisted 'Ready to proceed', we moved gingerly forward until the strain was on the tow, and this odd procession of cripples set course for the Shetlands, our nearest friendly land.

I felt particularly naked, because it would take some moments to slip the tow and, by then, we had heard that the enemy concentrated a large force of U-boats in the North Sea, all too ready to receive our 'surprise' liberation of Norway. However, we had a quiet passage and had made a good landfall by the time the *Zulu* got a submarine contact ahead. The U-boat, one of the small 250-tonners, was rash enough to surface for a few seconds. The *Zulu* did not have time to ram, but carried out a good attack, and if the U-boat was not sunk, it was badly shaken.

We then took the *Kashmir* in to Lerwick harbour, topped up with fuel and, together with the *Zulu*, sailed to join the fleet before dark — leaving two extremely disconsolate ships' companies to argue about who had been wrong.

The Germans in order to secure the Swedish iron ore and the Allies in order to forestall them had both planned to invade Norway simultaneously. The German plan was bold, thorough and resolutely executed. Ours was hesitant and hedged with restrictions on dealing with the Norwegians if they showed opposition. It was carried out with little determination by the High Command and the result was inevitable. The Germans were soon in possession of the main Norwegian ports and airfields, while Allied activity was restricted to rather ineffective minelaying. Our submarines did great work in the Skagerrak, but other results were disappointing.

There was now an uneasy pause while the ships cruised up and down the coast waiting for decisions in Whitehall. However, life was by no means dull, and we spent the next three days screening various battleships, battlecruisers and aircraft-carriers, who were cruising up and down the Norwegian coast waiting for the German big ships to appear. There was not much darkness, we spent an hour or more at each dawn and dusk at action stations, and there were numerous alarms of every sort. In addition we were all, officers and men, in two watches. This meant that sleep was precious and life a mechanical rotation of watch, sleep and eat, with only periods at action stations to break the monotony.

The fleet was bombed twice while we were present; we saw the *Escapade* hit and the *York* very near-missed, and some splinters came inboard. The ships were well out of shore-based fighter protection, and the aircraft-carrier fighters were far too busy trying to protect their own machines to help. The Doctor, who was taking his first experience of action very seriously, insisted on laying out the tools of his trade permanently on the wardroom table — a display which, mixing poorly with the cottage pies and welsh rarebits to which we were by then reduced, provided a grim reminder of what might be in store.

I know now, and we had a shrewd idea then, that the area was stiff with U-boats; but, by the Grace of God, none of them succeeded in hitting any of our warships. Their depth keeping was poor, and many good shots which should have exploded on impact missed by passing underneath. To add to their troubles the magnetic, proximity-fuze pistols were defective and the contact pistols only went off if the angle of incidence was near ninety degrees — so some torpedoes which hit, bounced off their targets.

In his book, Admiral Doenitz estimates, after a careful analysis, that if the torpedoes had functioned correctly, one out of the four attacks on capital ships would have been successful, seven out of the twelve on cruisers, seven out of the ten on destroyers and all five of those made on troopships. This would have been a disaster to the Allies which is horrible to contemplate.

Despite urgent investigation by the German experts, the reasons for these failures were not finally established until January 1942, and then by accident. A U-boat in the middle of the Atlantic was carrying out an unauthorized inspection of one of its torpedoes and discovered a leak in the depth-keeping compartment. A report was made by radio at once, but even then it was not till December 1942 that all U-boats at sea had efficient torpedoes. This was a most surprising failure by the German technical people, who were normally competent and thorough. It seems to have been due to a combination of over-confidence and refusal to listen to reports from sea.

One or two incidents emerge with clearness from this hazy background: The difficulty we had in getting the two-pounder

Pom Pom to stop firing at Heinkels at 15,000 feet; our excitement when the *Renown* rejoined after her long chase of the *Scharnhorst* and the *Gneisenau*, both of whom she routed at the cost of a shell through the midshipmen's study and the loss of the navigator's big toe; screening the two big ships while Admiral Whitworth transferred with his staff from the *Renown* to the *Warspite* in a cutter on a dark night with a long swell; screening the *Furious* while she flew off two flights of Swordfish and Skuas for an attack with torpedoes and bombs on the enemy ships in Narvik and Trondheim; and the signal which was passed around the screening destroyers giving the result of the attack, and the number of aircraft missing. And, above all, the patient calm of the Captain, who never got excited, never became irritable, and never shouted, 'What is the delay, First Lieutenant?' when a job was taking too long.

Then came news of the first battle of Narvik, on 10th April, where Captain Warburton-Lee's flotilla had attacked with great skill and gallantry a much superior force of German destroyers in Narvik Fjord. He had caught them by surprise before dawn and had inflicted heavy casualties but at the cost of two of his force, and his own life, in this great venture.

We all knew that something was bound to turn up for us to do. We were not far wrong. After much shilly-shallying both in Whitehall and by the authorities on the spot, an attack on the destroyers still remaining in Narvik was organized, though there was an unnecessary delay. If, on the day after the first battle, an immediate attack had been mounted, the enemy would have been found completely disorganized and incapable of serious resistance. As it was, the ships were given time during this two-day delay to prepare a hot reception. Fortunately, the German senior officer remaining — the Commodore had been killed in the first battle — was equally dilatory and missed an easy chance, as he had been ordered, of slipping out and escaping.

Accordingly, by noon, 13th April, we were steaming past the fort at the entrance to Narvik Fjord, in company with eight other destroyers, three of whom had their minesweeps out, and followed, at a respectful distance, by the *Warspite*. Not being certain whether the Germans had manned the fort, we trained all guns on it as we passed, and also there were rumours of a controlled minefield. But we got by safely, with sighs of relief. It would be unfortunate if the *Warspite* bought a mine, but not disastrous, as we could get on well without her and, to tell the truth, we small ships rather resented the fact that a 'wagon' was coming in too. We felt her to be more of a liability than an asset anyhow, although her Swordfish seaplane was of great value later on.

I remember arranging with the Petty Officer Cook for vast supplies of corned-beef sandwiches and tea for all quarters, and also sending down to the messman for sandwiches for the officers. As usual, Camilleri did us proud and soon a voluble Maltese was distributing beer and plates of excellent sandwiches on the bridge. The word had already been passed about clean underclothes; there was plenty of ready-use ammunition at the guns; we knew that there were at least eight enemy destroyers ahead of us; and we felt entirely confident of the result, although most were glad of the food to stop a severe sinking feeling in the pit of the stomach.

So far all had gone well on board except for one bad slip-up. The Yeoman of Signals found that he had no full-sized ensigns to hoist as battle ensigns and we were forced to improvise with boats' ensigns, which looked the size of a pocket handkerchief — an ignominious alternative. But I was glad of the opportunity of passing the tense minutes of waiting in telling the Yeoman exactly what I thought of him and his signalmen.

It was an astonishing scene. The fjord was narrow and deep, and the grey-green water was so smooth that the wakes left by the ships could be seen rippling away to the rocky shores. On both sides there were high mountains, on the slopes of which pine trees emerged starkly from the snow which covered the ground. The visibility was patchy, with promise of light rain to come, and the long line of ships stretched out in the mist, each one astern of the floats of the sweeping destroyers.

There were nine destroyers present, the three ships with mine-sweeping gear leading in the centre, the *Hero*, *Icarus* and the *Forester*, with the *Bedouin*, the *Punjabi* and the *Eskimo* on the starboard side and with the *Cossack*, *Kimberley* and the *Foxhound* to port.

As the force, for we could not be described as anything else being a collection of odd ships from some six different flotillas, passed the narrows, sweeps were got in and the formation opened out. Shortly afterwards the leading ship flashed a sighting report to the Senior Officer, *Bedouin*, who replied by hoisting the only signal which he made throughout the engagement. It was a single flag signal meaning, 'Open fire and engage the enemy'. What a model of brevity! We then caught a glimpse of one or two big German destroyers in the mist ahead, and within a few minutes we had fired a few salvoes from the foremost mountings with the object of finding the range. The after mountings, of course, would not then bear.

After the first salvoes had been fired, events became blurred in my memory. There was the *Warspite*'s Swordfish flying past on its way to reconnoitre Narvik and its return with a report that it had sunk a U-boat in Herjangs Fjord and with exact news of the enemy positions; in particular the fact that there was one destroyer beached in Djupvik Bay on the starboard side of the fjord and another secured to a jetty inside Narvik harbour covering the entrance. We saw also some big aircraft flying in formation over the hills to northward — they must have been enemy, but either they did not see us or else they were not interested.

Then the leading ships began to be straddled by the enemy fire, which was not nearly so accurate or so rapid as I had expected. We did not then know they had been unable to top up fully after the first battle because the flotilla of 'H's led by Captain Warburton-Lee in the *Hardy* had sunk their ammunition supply ship before it reached Narvik.

The force had automatically spread over the fjord and was zig-zagging to and fro independently to avoid the gunfire and to allow the after guns to bear; it advanced in two rough lines abreast. We were well over to port and therefore missed the slaughter of the sitting bird in the bay to starboard. But she burst into flames very quickly without us and the *Warspite* completed her destruction with some rounds of fifteen-inch. The thunder of the *Warspite*'s opening salvo took us by surprise. Owing to her distance astern, by the time the noise had reached us the cordite smoke of her salvoes had cleared away, leaving no apparent source of the sound. It seemed at first as if a ship had blown up astern.

The leading ship, the *Hero*, was guide, and could not zig-zag; she had to steer a steady course and speed down the fjord. But although she was constantly straddled, she was never hit, both to her and our surprise.

Then the German destroyers started firing torpedoes down the fjord. The tracks were quite easy to see, and one or two were giving poor performances, 'porpoising' badly. But it was easier to see them than to avoid them. Nine ships zigging across a narrow fjord do not help independent avoiding action! The fish must have been set deep to hit the *Warspite*, or else the magnetic pistols were defective, because I sighted one track coming from about fifty yards off our port beam and watched it pass under the foremost funnel. An awkward moment in which all the rules about flexing knees and biting rubber flashed through the mind. Many torpedoes were fired but none hit. Surely no finer target has ever been given than a battleship in a narrow fjord!

There were also U-boats around, and Commander Topp, who later became a U-boat ace and who was serving at the time as an officer in U-49, gives an exciting account of the action from the submarine point of view.

In the course of a most interesting account of his boat's adventures in Narvik and Ofot fjords, he describes how U-49, with two torpedoes ready, was in an excellent position to fire at the *Warspite* as she came steaming up the fjord. The U-boat passed under the destroyer screen without detection and was about to fire when it hit a pinnacle rock. In the efforts to get off the bottom, it came up too quick, and Topp says that the fore end of the boat broke surface. I do not remember any report of a surfaced submarine, but be that as it may, an attacking chance had been lost and the *Warspite* went by unscathed.

I had stationed myself in the port corner of the bridge abaft the 'clear view screen', the naval equivalent of a windscreen wiper, behind which I ducked whenever the whine of a salvo was heard in the air. The navigator bravely took photographs of the shell splashes and caught one or two close ones; but the results were disappointing. In the photographs they look miles away.

We had our first casualty about then, when a salvo of two fell alongside, and splinters hit the gunlayer of the Pom Pom, as well as making a very large number of holes in the ship's side by the mess decks — flooding one of them to a depth of about a foot. Water started to leak into the magazines and shell rooms below, but the crews, who consisted of two Maltese stewards in one and the Petty Officer Cook and a Maltese cook in the other, were unperturbed — once they had been assured, by voice pipe, that there was not too much water above their heads. Those supply parties did a fine job. Like the engine room and boiler-room teams, they never knew what was happening above, and could only listen for the explosion, hoping for the best. It is much more fun to slam a shell into a gun and to be able to look about. Then you float off, too.

This same near-miss sent large quantities of water over the ship, drenching us all on the bridge. I shall never forget the taste of the cordite-contaminated water. That taste, and the smell of the superstructure near our shell hits, are my most vivid memories. We were straddled sixteen times in ten minutes during this part of the battle, but then the action got to rather closer range and we began to hit them hard. The mist made gunnery difficult and observation of splashes impossible at long range but, when we got closer, it was soon clear that we had little to fear. The *Warspite* started to throw shells towards the shore batteries at Narvik about then too, and the situation got very confused. The enemy were zigging to and fro as we were, but retreating all the time, and it was easy to change targets without knowing it; with the result that I had some entertaining passages with the control officer on the gunnery telephone.

Then, very suddenly, we seemed to be off Narvik itself, which has a narrow entrance on the south side of the fjord dominated by a hill on which we could see a gun. As a result of Fleet Air Arm reconnaissance before the start of the operation, we had been detailed by *Bedouin* to enter the harbour itself and to destroy all shipping there; while the remainder of the destroyers followed the enemy up the next fjord, Rombaks. Accordingly, we ceased firing, had a quick check up of the gunnery instruments and altered over to starboard to approach the entrance.

We passed very close on our port hand the burning hulk of a Leberecht Maas-class destroyer and the Huns could be seen jumping into the water from both sides of her. The *Punjabi* was busy finishing her off and we did not interfere, to the fury of the Torpedo Gunner who was desperately keen to fire his precious charges. He ran up to the bridge and made a pathetic appeal to the Captain, who, rightly, wished to keep them for other game.

To take his mind off the subject I asked the Torpedo Gunner what he thought of our gunnery, and we became so engrossed in our criticism, both destructive and bawdy, that the Captain told us, rather acidly, to shut up and pay attention to the next item on the programme.

There was a nasty moment when the ship nearly ran down two swimmers, who were shouting 'Help!' We thought they might be Swordfish survivors, for we knew that one machine was missing. But we could not stop in any case, and our minds were put at rest by their Teutonic abuse as we passed them by.

The report from the *Warspite*'s Swordfish had warned us that we would probably meet some opposition on rounding the point at the entrance to the harbour, so the guns were trained on the port bow; and everything was on the top line to open fire with minimum delay. Narvik harbour opened out into an enclosed anchorage, and the hill at the entrance prevented any view from outside of the ships alongside the jetties of the town, which were on the left-hand or northern shore.

The ship passed the bend at about twelve knots, for the harbour was littered with the wrecks left there after the visit of Captain Warburton-Lee's flotilla and a higher speed would have been madness. 'B' gun deck reported the enemy first, then we at the fore end of the bridge sighted her, and almost immediately the director's crew were able to see her as the ship slid past the point.

Crack! — both ships opened fire together, I think we were a little before them if anything — and at a range of under a mile, we scored a clean miss short with our first salvo. The Germans made no mistake, however, and two or three 5.1 shells burst against the ship's side forrard of the bridge. But we did not repeat our error with the next salvo nor with the following one, and the enemy had only time to fire two or three more salvoes before she became a silently burning wreck. Our smaller shells seemed to have a devastating effect, whereas theirs made a big hole in the side but did not penetrate much farther.

After our first salvo, 'A' mounting had ceased firing and the Captain told me to find out what was the trouble. I could get no answer from the telephone, so rather reluctantly I left my snug corner and ran down to 'B' gun deck, thence jumping from the flare on to 'A' gun shield, from where I could get a good look round. 'B' mounting's crew had several wounded but were keeping going well, and the Leading Seaman, captain of the gun, grinned at me as I passed and seemed to have the situation well in hand. 'A' gun's crew had several wounded too and seemed in rather a dazed state, because one shell had burst at the fore end of the petty officers' mess within a few feet of them, killing most of the supply parties inside; while another had burst in the mess deck below and had effectually stopped all supply to the forrard guns. Unlike 'B' gun's crew, however, they were hanging around waiting for an order. A word to 'Get cracking on the ready-use ammunition on deck' soon put them in action again.

On returning to the bridge to report, the first thing I noticed was a neat hole where a splinter had passed through my clear view screen. We had been hit several times while I was forrard, the bridge was full of splinter holes, another shell had exploded on a funnel guy and it was increasingly evident that all was not well below. The wheelhouse reported 'Ship will not answer the wheel', and despite the fact that the telegraphs had been put to full speed astern, we were firmly heading for the shore at the south side of the harbour.

By some chance, the ship dodged the wrecks, although there were some close shaves, and we grounded, bows on to a steeply shelving beach on the opposite side of the harbour to our opponent. It was now time to investigate the situation generally.

A semi-armour-piercing shell had exploded in the foremost boiler room, instantly killing the crew, cutting all leads from the bridge to the steering engine and to the telegraphs, and fracturing the main steam pipe, so that the engines were temporarily useless and the ship could not be steered. We had eight hits in all, none abaft the boiler room. There seemed to be a fire forrard on the lower mess decks and the fore end of the ship was full of smoke. There I met the Gunnery Control Officer, who had left his director tower as all the electrical circuits had been shot away, and he flooded the forrard magazine. We were taking no risks, although now I fear that there was more smoke than flame about that fire. It was then that I blessed our drill of walking about the ship in a smoke helmet blindfolded, as we found little difficulty in making our way about the smoke-filled spaces. There have been some unpleasant accidents under similar circumstances. Indeed, one man got very excited and was running around screaming, but luckily a flooding wheel spanner was handy and he was soon quiet. Otherwise the behaviour of the whole ship's company was admirable.

There were about twelve killed and rather more wounded — a surprisingly small number considering the punishment we had taken. I went again on to the bridge to report, to find the Engineer Officer there in discussion with the Captain.

The harbour was quiet for the moment and we made a quick plan of campaign. The Chief was going to isolate the forrard boiler room and get steam and electrical power back as soon as possible. The doctor, ably assisted by the flotilla schoolmaster, was doing great work in taking the wounded aft. They settled the worst cases in the Captain's cabin and the sick bay which were on the upper deck, the next ones in the officers' cabins below, and the lighter cases in the ward-room. We had no time to move the dead; they had to wait till later.

The flotilla schoolmaster was in great form. He had kept an excellent narrative of events during the action, and now, arrayed in the plus-fours which he had insisted on wearing during his first engagement, was doing the work of three men.

I left the Pom Pom and a couple of 4.7-inch mountings manned, while the remainder of the hands put out the fires, started to shift shells and other weights from forward to aft to lighten the bows and, under the supervision of Guns, prepared to be towed from aft. We hoped that someone would try to come to haul us off later.

The Gunnery Control Officer took a party to put tingles over the holes in the first whaler, which was the only boat which looked like being repairable. Eventually they lowered it and sounded astern in order to pick out a suitable avenue of retreat, unobstructed by hidden wrecks.

The officer in charge of confidential books had an appalling job. The ship was in an invidious position. We did not know whether we should be able to get her off, nor when this would happen. There had been many German soldiers in Narvik the day before and, although it was quiet now, they might come back to find a sitting target. In addition we had sighted a number of bombers flying around which certainly did not belong to us. So the Captain decided to burn all confidential and signal books, and the Signal Officer and a Leading Telegraphist spent a pleasant few hours tearing up the products of days of work and correction in order to fling them into the boiler-room furnace.

The Petty Officer Telegraphist was busy re-rigging aerials, which had all been shot away, and the Petty Officer Cook was hard at work in the galley.

We still had our objective to achieve, which was the destruction of all shipping in the harbour. Two or three ships of various nationalities were still floating alongside the iron-ore jetty; so we started to fill them with high-explosive shells in a rather cold-blooded manner. About that time, too, an occasional rifle bullet would come pinging past the ship. We stopped that game by sending a burst from the Pom Pom in the general direction of each shot.

We were getting a little excited by then, and the guns' crews were taking too much advantage of this glorious opportunity of plastering a town at no expense. There was hardly a prominent building in sight in which some keen-eyed enthusiast did not spot a sniper, usually imaginary, and it was necessary to damp their ardour. 'This is an Allied town,' they were told firmly, and also, 'Keep clear of that hospital on the hill,' where we could see the flag of the Red Cross flying. It was a happy coincidence that, together with some German wounded, there were in that hospital several survivors from the *Hunter*, including an old friend of mine who was First Lieutenant.

A Norwegian on skis came down to the waterside to tell us that the survivors from the *Hardy* were in a village a few miles down the fjord, and also that all the Germans had fled the town for the hills.

We were very keen to land and take the town and we made a signal to the Admiral asking permission so to proceed. Platoons were reorganized, rifles collected, and carley rafts prepared for towing by the whaler. I had selected my headquarters in a likely looking pub on the waterfront, and I was busy discussing 'strong-points', 'enfilading fire' and other mysteries with the Lewis-gun section, when news came that our request to land had not been approved. It was disappointing, for in addition to the fun, I would have been damn glad to get clear of the ship — a fact, I would never have admitted at the time — and what is more, I am convinced that we could have held the town until the soldiers arrived.

The evidence available since the war seems to support our theory. The then Mayor of Narvik, in his book *The Mountains Wait*, describes the morale of the soldiers ashore as very poor and the sailors from the sunken destroyers who were to fight so well as a naval battalion had not had time to get together. Moreover, there were British soldiers in troopships not far off — admittedly they were not ready for an assault for their heavy equipment was not with them — but men with rifles was all that was required. This was another example of a lack of boldness in the High Command which at the start of the war, and in contrast to the Germans, missed so many good chances.

Some time before our whaler was fit to lower — when, I am not certain, as time meant little that day — the *Foxhound* entered the harbour and sent over her doctor to help us with the wounded, also sending a boat to board the destroyer which we had left burning alongside the jetty. Their whaler was greeted with a burst of machine-gun fire and wisely withdrew. The *Foxhound* opened fire with her 4.7's and quite soon blew up the Hun's magazines. We heard afterwards that this ship, the *Roeder*, had been damaged in the first battle, and could not steam, having been left as harbour defence ship with gun crews only on board. The rest of the crew had been sent to replace casualties in other ships in their flotilla.

The lack of enterprise by the German soldiery had been for some time too good to last. A few moments later there was the noise of a gun firing, followed by a largish splash in the water close to the shore. About a minute later, there was another splash about ten yards closer to us and it was only too clear that the enemy was using a howitzer. If we did not stop them, it was only a matter of time before we were hit — and hit continually. All binoculars were used to search in the direction of the sound; and quite soon, well visible against the snow, we saw a small group of men silhouetted against the snow on a hill at the back of the town. Was it possible that they were fools enough to be using direct fire when they could easily fire from behind the ridge in perfect safety? Apparently this was so, and 'B' mounting was trained on the group. I took over gun layer myself, as I did not want any mistakes over identification. After a good deal of 'train left — left — no the other left, you bloody fool', we got on the target with a good estimated range.

The first rounds went whizzing over the top of the ridge and were never seen again. We saw the second two fall quite close and the third or fourth salvos must have hit, because the howitzer never fired again. This result was due more to good luck than skill, and I then really understood what 'backlash' meant. The backlash of the sights was enormous after a long day's firing and several large dents in the gun shield, and consecutive rounds sighted on exactly the same point of aim fell a long way from each other. But we were highly delighted, as the last few enemy shells had been so close they had splashed water inboard.

It was also good news when the Chief reported that the engines were ready with two boilers, and that he had pumped a good deal of water out of the flooded spaces forrard. Having finished shifting all movable weight aft, the Captain sent a signal to the *Kimberley* to say that we were ready to be towed.

The *Kimberley* put her bow very close to our stern, lowered a wire down on to our quarter deck, and we were ready in a very short time. All hands were mustered aft, our engines were put to half and then full astern and the *Kimberley* started to tug stern first. To help move the ship off the ground, we did some rhythmic jumping aft, an exhibition which made us feel self-conscious and seemed to do little good. The *Kimberley* tugged away, our screws were revolving fast and the stern was moving up and down with our efforts, but still the two trees on the beam which I was using as a transit stayed steady. We seemed stuck for good.

Then came some more fobbing about with tide tables, with the result that it was decided to try again early next morning when the tide was highest, although there was but little rise and fall. The *Kimberley* left harbour and the work of clearing up the ship and preparing for sea continued.

There was one more scare before dark. Another blazing German wreck was drifting down the middle of the fjord, past which we saw a destroyer steaming, trying evidently to finish it off. Then there was a tremendous explosion on the shore a little way to the westward of where we were beached, which sent the guns' crews to their stations to repel aircraft. But we could see no aircraft, and only when we received 'Sorry' from the offender did we realize that, at point-blank range, she had missed the wreck with a torpedo which had exploded on the shore.

By dark we were all exhausted and the tot of rum all round was most welcome. Men were falling asleep all over the upper deck, for the mess decks were uninhabitable; and the cabins were filled with wounded.

After dark I took the whaler to the *Punjabi* to transfer some of the wounded who were fit to be moved. Then I slept, leaving a scanty guard on watch. There was a possibility of our being boarded but we were so tired that it did not seem important, and, anyhow, we were all lying ready on the upper deck armed to the teeth.

About half an hour before the time I had asked to be called, a quartermaster woke me up and said, 'I think she's afloat, sir.' I leaped up and found he was quite right. Luckily, as there was no wind, we were still bows on. I called the Captain, who rang down to the engine room at once; we weighed both anchors, which had been dropped under foot to lighten her, hoisted the whaler and steamed thankfully out stern first — the whaler's chart of the wrecks proving particularly useful.

Soon after daylight, which was very early, we closed the *Warspite*, making a good alongside stern first, for we could not risk putting any strain on the compartments forward by moving ahead. The *Warspite* was steaming at about six knots. The remaining wounded were soon transferred, and we cast off and set out for a fjord in the Lofoten Islands which provided a good sheltered anchorage where the oilers and repair ships were to assemble.

The wounded behaved well. Some of them were badly burnt, most of them were in great pain, but the two doctors worked like Trojans and, with liberal doses of morphia, made them as comfortable as possible. How I blessed that morphia. The screams and moans of the wounded are ghastly to hear, and quickly destroy the best morale, but fortunately the drug had an immediate effect.

Before we let go, the Admiral came to his quarter deck and talked to our Captain. We learned that all eight of the enemy ships had been destroyed at the cost of damage to the *Eskimo*, when she led the way through the narrow entrance to Rombaks Fjord, into which the enemy had retreated like cornered rats in a hole. A torpedo had blown her bows off when she appeared in view, causing heavy casualties in killed and missing; but there had been only light losses in the other ships. It was a satisfactory revenge for the first battle, when the *Hardy* and the *Hunter* had been lost and many killed and wounded. In addition, the *Warspite*'s Swordfish had sunk U-64, which was lying at anchor in the fjord, with a direct hit.

Once clear of the *Warspite*, I remember going down to my cabin which still showed traces of a badly wounded man, and, happening to catch a glimpse of myself in a mirror, I realized why some of the *Warspite*'s crew had stared. A filthy black face confronted me, unshaven and covered with streaks of blood from the wounded whom we had carried below. A quick clean-up was followed by a breakfast fit for a king. Old Spiteri, the cook, was a rascal over whom I had no control whatever, who only stopped moaning to answer back in highly insubordinate Maltese; but he never failed to produce a good meal whatever the conditions. The officers had been luckier than the ship's company, because their cabins, mess and store rooms were intact; whereas the mess decks were not habitable and most of the provision rooms and the refrigerator had been flooded. Corned beef and biscuit was a standing meal forrard until we were able to bake some bread and scrounge some meat from other ships.

When I went up on deck, I found that we were steering from aft and that the weather was fine with only a slight chop, which threw spray over the quarter deck as we pushed into the sea.

The Chief Bosun's Mate and I spent a hurried half-hour reorganizing the watch bill; and then the hands turned-to in order to prepare for entering 'Cripple's Creek', as our fjord was soon named. I had one unpleasant duty still to arrange: the preparation for burial. Some volunteers were found who completed the task by not long after noon. After dinner, when we were in sight of our destination, all hands were mustered on the foc'sle. A guard of honour had been provided from the few men on board who had not lost their kit, and their uniforms and shaven faces contrasted strangely with the duffle-coats, overalls and haggard appearance of the remainder.

The Captain left the bridge to read the simple service; the guard presented arms, and twelve hammock-covered forms slid over the side. There were few on board who were not assisting at their first burial at sea; it was an impressive moment, and caused all of us to think hard.

I was lucky to have been such a short time in the ship and had not known the men who had been killed, so I could feel more impersonal about the losses.

The Captain returned to the bridge, the guard marched off, and before anyone could have time to think too much, the pipe 'Hands prepare for entering harbour' had sent the ship's company to their various jobs.

Half an hour later we were passing the entrance to the fjord bound for the anchorage where several ships were lying. 'Hello, what's the crowd on the *Zulu*'s foc'sle? My word, they have caught us bending, I believe they are going to cheer us.' There was not time to get the hands together to answer the cheers, but the situation was saved by the inevitable wit, who, leaning far out of the biggest of the shell-holes in the side, shouted, 'Three weeks leave to each watch for this lot.'

Then we let go the anchor, squared up the ship and, by evening, a proud but tired team were all down to a thousand fathoms, enjoying their first night's rest for over a week. Having joined the ship on a Friday and sailed for Norway on the following Sunday, I had a brisk introduction to my new duties. I was very lucky in that the *Cossack* had been in commission for some time and had kept many experienced officers and men who had been in the ship from the start and knew her and their jobs backwards.

Next day the work of clearing up continued, and with the help of canvas over the holes it was possible to make the mess decks a little less uncomfortable. Chief made a thorough survey of the damage, while as much water as could be reached was pumped overboard, because it was necessary also to lighten the ship forrard in order to get the lowest shell-hole out of the water. This was soon done; and a repair conference was held, at which a Norwegian civil engineer from ashore was present. Neither the tools nor plates for the job being available on board, arrangements were made with a local firm of building contractors to do the work, and the following day a team of tough and enthusiastic Norwegians arrived alongside the ship. How they worked! It was bitterly cold but they seemed not to notice, and their only requirements were food and hot drink in very large quantities. They would arrive in a little steamer from a neighbouring fjord at dawn each day, not returning home until dusk, so working over twelve hours without complaint. If the Gestapo did not get at them, I hope that we were able to show our gratitude after the war.

Indeed, we met nothing but kindness from these hardy northerners, and the hospital ashore took great care of the wounded from the *Hotspur* and the *Hasty*, which were lying in the fjord when we arrived. In addition, the *Penelope* was beached at the end of the fjord with severe damage to her bottom; and others of the destroyers who were taking part in the Norwegian campaign kept entering and leaving harbour. There was also a German merchant ship, which had been captured by a destroyer not long before. Her scuttling charges had been badly placed, so an enterprising boarding party had stuffed the holes with mattresses and steamed her back. It so happened that the destroyer Captain recognized the German master as an officer in the *Bremen*, in which he had taken passage before the war, and with whose officers he had become friendly! This ship was full of stores and was of great value to us.

The next arrival was the *Eskimo*, who also entered stern first. She looked a sad sight forrard and, of course, could not anchor because there were neither anchors nor cable left. She was therefore berthed alongside the German, whose derricks were used to lift out 'B' mounting, which was perched precariously forward. Then came a fleet oiler which was in continual use; next a net layer, which layed its nets across the entrance as a protection against submarines; and the advent of the repair ship *Vindictive* completed a self-contained base.

The time passed quickly at first, there being much to do about the ship. We transferred ammunition to one ship, the *Zulu*, and torpedoes to another, the *Bedouin*. The fjord was within bombing range of German-held aerodromes, so that it was necessary to keep the high-angle armament constantly manned. But after a week it began to be difficult to find occupation for the ship's company, who could not all be employed about the repairs, and we were pleased to send working parties to other ships to help with storing and like jobs.

The small planing motor-dinghy, or 'skimming dish' as it was called, was repaired, and on several fine afternoons we explored the neighbouring fjords which were very beautiful when the sun shone on the snow-covered mountains around them. At one village we met some delightful children, who duly came off to have tea on board. They were wildly excited by the trip, enjoying most, I think, the hooded duffle-coats which we lent them for the boat journey. Let us hope that they have not suffered since.

The next fjord was crowded with Eider duck which were so tame that it was difficult to avoid running them down in the boat. It was a pity that they were not fit to eat. We got plenty of fresh fish, however, from the fishing boats which came alongside daily, so on the whole we could have been much worse off.

Then a German snooper was sighted flying over the fjord at a great height, and we felt that the sooner we were away, the better! The repair team finished their work and we were ready to go, leaving the *Penelope* and the *Eskimo* to face the inevitable — which arrived next day in the form of a squadron of Heinkels, who carried out daily bombing practice on their helpless targets. Luckily they never hit, although there were a few casualties from splinters, and both ships followed us home to fight again.

We sailed as the official escort of the oiler, who had, by then, exhausted her fuel. I say 'official', as our bows were still on the shaky side, and we were only capable of slow speed in anything other than a flat calm. Perhaps we were sent together according to the theory that 'two is company' — it was comforting to have a companion!

We met some bad weather soon after reaching the North Sea, with the result that the compartments forward began to 'pant' as the ship pitched into the sea, slowly filling up with water. Those were the days before portable pumps in destroyers; the suction line would not reach the spot, so a bucket chain was organized which worked continually for three days, until the weather improved. It was heart-breaking and tiring work, for every time the bows fell into a heavy trough there was a rush of water, undoing the work of the last few minutes.

It was then that the really tough and determined men stood out from their fellows, and those who stood out were not always the ones of whom we expected the best.

There was only one other excitement. One afternoon, in perfect visibility, the mast of a big ship was sighted over the horizon ahead. No news of any big ship movements had been received, so we were not sure whether she was friend or foe. The alarm bells were rung, but the *Warspite*'s familiar outline soon appeared above the horizon and the ship's company thankfully left their action stations.

A few days later the ship was safely in dock at Southampton and repairs were quickly under way.

3. INVASION SEASON

THE *Cossack*'s repairs were completed just after Dunkirk. It was exactly the wrong time for us, because all officers and men are required on board for the last week before sailing; and none of us could get away to join the show at Dover. The ships lying near us, which were not due to complete for some time, all sent parties which took boats and other craft of every description to the beaches.

Our flotilla leader had been bombed and sunk off Norway, and we were chosen for the honour of carrying Captain D 4 and his staff. This meant many changes in the ship and considerable work before the staff were all settled in. We also lost our Captain, who went to another ship. At the last moment, a twin four-inch anti-aircraft gun of the same excellent type as I had had in the *Vega* was put on board, and we sailed with workmen still busy putting in the last bolts and finishing off the electrical circuits. We lost one 4.7-inch low-angle mounting, but the exchange was well worth while, as many ships sunk at Dunkirk would testify. We were not destined to carry out gun trials! At such a time, every hour was critical, and we left to rejoin the fleet at high speed, drilling the gun's crew on the way up to Scapa Flow.

There was only time to top up with fuel on arrival, before we were out again, screening part of the fleet which was carrying out one of the periodical sweeps towards the Norwegian coast. Our new pair of guns soon had a chance to show their value. The force was seen by a Dornier flying-boat not long after sailing; in those days, there was but one possible consequence to the sight of that sinister shape low over the horizon. A brief calculation of the distance to the nearest base; and we were able to warn the hands when they were likely to go to 'action stations'.

It was a helpless feeling to watch the flying-boat wandering up and down, always well out of gun range. We could not be reached by shore fighters, and no aircraft-carrier, whose planes would shoot down the shadower, was available.

Our estimate was right within five minutes, and everything was ready when the first bombers were sighted, dodging in and out of high cloud. The Huns had not taken long to get their striking force off the ground, and their 'homing' was perfect. The planes were Heinkel IIIs, which were to be so familiar to the south coast a few months later. They made one or two runs, but the bombing was poor and no ships were hit.

It was not long before we were within fighter range and the sight of Spitfires in the sky sent the enemy hareing for home.

Before we got back, the four-inch had fired well over a hundred rounds from each gun, the gun's crew had become a first-class team, and the mounting had had a most thorough trial!

At that time, during the summer of 1940, the fleet was in its weakest state. The Norwegian campaign, the invasion of the Low Countries, and Dunkirk, had produced heavy losses, mostly by aircraft. The Italians had just entered the war, making a reinforcement of the fleet in the Mediterranean necessary, and new ships were coming out very slowly.

There was little offensive activity, therefore, except by the Fleet Air Arm and by the submarines, who were badly hampered by enemy air activity; and the fleet was reduced to waiting at Scapa Flow for the enemy to make a move, and to carrying out many exercises.

One night in July, however, there was an alarm. A little before midnight, a signal to raise steam with all dispatch was received, and two hours later we were leading the flotilla through the boom gate. That short sentence describes a multitude of events. While steam was being hurriedly raised in the boilers, the engines were being warmed through, the boats were being hoisted, two bridles of cable were being unshackled from the buoy to which we were secured, and the ship was being prepared for sea by lashing down the innumerable pieces which can be so dangerous in a seaway.

The reason for this 'panic' sailing was a signal from the submarine *Shark* which had reported that she had been damaged close to the Norwegian coast, and was unable to dive, and required help at once. A strong force of cruisers and destroyers were sent out to try to find her, and were making high speed towards her estimated position by dawn. Some Blenheims, too, were to be sent out to help the search. I was particularly interested in this operation, because the First Lieutenant of the submarine was an old friend and I was all the more anxious that it should be successful.

A little after dawn we were near the position where we expected to find her but, despite good visibility, there was nothing to be seen. Contact was made with one of the Blenheims, who reported that he also had seen nothing and then went off for a final sweep of the area. If aircraft had failed to sight her, the ships would be very unlikely to do so, and the Admiral ordered a retirement. This move was a popular one, for we were uncomfortably close to the aerodromes near Trondheim and Stavanger, which was to be shown only too soon.

The ships had been spread out some distance apart in order to increase the chance of sighting the submarine or any survivors from it, and each depended, therefore, on her own armament for protection. Shortly after we had turned back, aircraft were reported astern and four or five machines could be seen flying low towards the ship. It was difficult to see what they were, but all were twin-engined and might have been British or German. As they got nearer, we could see that there was some sort of fight going on, and soon our guns opened fire. Recognition was very difficult, and the confusion of the melee indescribable. It will never be known whether we or the Germans hit them, but within a few seconds two Blenheims had crashed in flames — one close to us, and the other, which another destroyer attended to, about a mile away. The other three aircraft flew off.

The sheet of flames which shot up from the plane when it hit the water made the chance of any survivors from either seem small; but, to our amazement, three bodies were seen close to the burning wreckage, and a whaler was lowered which picked them up. One man was badly hurt and the other two shocked and shaken, and it was not an easy job to get them into the boat. But there were plenty of men on the boat's falls, and the speed at which we were hoisted made it seem as though we were in an express lift.

The planes had apparently been chased by a strong force of M.E.-110s, and had closed the ship in desperation. They had been badly damaged already, and the air crew did not resent the fact that our fire may have hit them — in fact, they were delighted to be saved. They had been astonishingly lucky, for out of the six men from both planes, only one, who broke his back in the crash, died, and the remainder were practically untouched.

We were pleased to be able to get under way again, because lying stopped with boats down within fighter range of the Hun was not healthy, and we knew that it would not be long before we saw more of the Luftwaffe.

The destroyers had hardly time to join the cruisers, who were some way to the west of us, when the Heinkels arrived. In contrast to our last outing, they had sent out their first team, and some bombs fell extremely close. We were plastered all the forenoon, and one destroyer on the screen was hit on the quarter deck — not seriously. A cordite fire, which was quickly put out, started among the ammunition on deck, but they were able to make a good twenty knots. The bombing was well organized. After each run the team concerned nipped back to base and took another load on board, to be back with us within a couple of hours. There were several teams out that day; and our high-angle guns were kept busy.

By the afternoon they were still hard at it, there was still a long way to go before we were in range of friendly fighters, and the problem of ammunition supply was getting serious. We had heard lurid stories, from friends who also had met trouble off Norway, of firing starshell and practice shell as a last resort when the live rounds had run out. Single-gun salvoes had just been ordered in order to economize ammunition, when a bank of fog was sighted ahead. Fog can be of doubtful advantage in these circumstances. If it is not high enough, the mast appears prominently out of the fog, giving the aircraft, who are invisible to the guns, a perfect target.

On this occasion all was well, and the bank remained thick and high all the way back to Scapa. It was hoped, of course, that the weather would clear before arrival; but this was not to be. To enter harbour at night in such visibility was impossible, and the force spent a most unpleasant time cruising up and down outside till the fog lifted.

Keeping in station was very difficult, and, owing to the high speed, the fog buoys which are towed astern to provide a mark for the next ship were useless. They were designed for lower speeds and not till much later did we get a fog buoy which 'watched' at all speeds. The ships were formed in two columns, steaming abreast of each other, with a cruiser leading each line. After one turn, disaster occurred. On our bridge we heard a noise like a bomb exploding. Enemy aircraft had been reported in the area only a few minutes before, and the first thought was that a big bomb had been dropped near by.

Then a signal was received saying that a cruiser had been in collision, and it was clear what the noise was. There had been some misunderstanding over a signal. On the turn a cruiser leading one of the columns had rammed a destroyer in the line astern, nearly cutting her in half amidships. A fire had broken out, and the next ship in the line was approaching to give what aid she could.

We could see nothing of this, of course, and continued in our line, until the signal was made to stop engines. In the meantime, the cruiser had backed out astern and lowered boats to pick up the survivors, and another destroyer had closed them and was doing the same. Fortunately there were not many casualties, but it had been an expensive night. Touch was lost with the hulk, and our flotilla spent a long forenoon the next day searching for it, until we were able to report that it had sunk.

From prisoners of war it was later learnt that the *Shark* had been caught on the surface, still unable to dive, by aircraft and by a force of trawlers. Rumour had it that they shot down one aircraft and accounted for a trawler before sinking, and that most of the survivors of this courageous company were picked up by the enemy.

After this episode of July 1940, the fleet spent a quiet time. For the first and last period of the war there was little seagoing, and we spent most of the time swinging round a buoy, always, of course, at short notice for getting under way.

Scapa is attractive only to those keen on walking and on bird life; and although I found plenty to do myself, the sailors generally did not get enough recreation. Facilities for games, concerts, and other amusements were practically non-existent, and to get to those affairs which were available, the men had a long and wet trip in an open boat. Boiler-cleaning periods were few, and, even then, we usually lay alongside our depot ship instead of going down to Rosyth where it was possible to give leave. To add to our troubles, a floating dock arrived one day, so that then even docking was no excuse to go south for a spell. It was a curious coincidence that the escort for this dock was taken from the East Coast convoy ships, and not from the Scapa destroyers!

But these were minor worries compared to the state of affairs brought on by the blitzes of the summer and autumn. Our crew came from the Portsmouth depot; many of them had homes there, and the town was getting badly bombed night after night. Even in peacetime Portsmouth ships are notoriously sensitive, and a gloom would be cast over the whole ship on each of the many Saturday evenings when 'Pompey' had lost at home. Now men's families were being wiped out and their homes destroyed, while we sat at our buoy helpless, without a single chance to get our own back.

Every morning crowds would listen to the seven o'clock news, and there were many requests for compassionate leave to deal with the tragedies of the bombing.

All nerves were on edge. Naturally, the men were difficult to handle; only action of some kind would put them right. It was ignominious to sit in our comfortable mess sipping a glass of sherry before sitting down to an excellent dinner, and then to read a letter from London or some other suffering city describing the horrors which the 'safe' civilians were facing with such courage. Our Captain was fully aware of all this. As a well-known fire-eater, I think he felt it worse than any of us, and before very long he was able to arrange a little outing to relieve the tension.

The Germans were running small coastal convoys of about half a dozen ships up and down the Norwegian coast to supply their garrisons there and to carry the iron-ore traffic from the north. These convoys were well covered by aircraft during daylight, but the surface escort was usually a weak one, consisting of a few trawlers and one or possibly two torpedo boats. After the Norwegian campaign, the Germans had few surface ships operational.

By using high speed, and by catching the convoy we wanted to attack in exactly the right place at the right time, a force of destroyers would be able to slip across the North Sea, using darkness as a cover during the dangerous part of the passage, hit the convoy hard off the Norwegian coast, and be back under the protection of shore fighters by daylight.

But it was necessary to wait till a convoy was passing a particular headland between certain hours of the night; the weather had to be such that high speed would be possible; and the wait, therefore, was a long one. Eventually, a reconnaissance by Coastal Command spotted a suitable north-bound convoy in the Skagerrak; our division of four Tribal destroyers sailed one afternoon, plans ready made for the attack.

The weather favoured us. The visibility was only moderate, the sea reasonably calm, and when night came no enemy ships or aircraft had spotted us. About twenty minutes before midnight we went to action stations; at fifteen minutes the flashing light on the headland for which we were steering was seen; and at five to twelve a large ship was sighted on the port bow.

We were leading the single line, and turned to port on to a parallel course to the enemy, followed by the other three destroyers, while the alarm signal was passed down the line.

The enemy could not have sighted us, since we got very close on their port quarters before fire was opened with guns and torpedoes. No one had challenged us, and there was a considerable delay before our fire was returned. They were massacred! All our ships fired starshell in whose light the convoy made a beautiful target. A small tanker was soon blazing furiously, and two more ships were on fire. Of the escorts there was little sign. The torpedo boat must have legged it towards the shore at high speed, and only a trawler was sighted, which sank quickly. When we had reached the head of the convoy, we led round and, followed by the remainder, gave the guns one more perfect run at the now sitting targets. After that, Captain D led off at high speed, for there was nothing to be gained by waiting, and the farther away from the Stavanger airfield we were by dawn the better off we should be.

I hope that that miserable escort returned to pick up survivors from the convoy. There was no time for us to do so. Everything had gone well. The simplicity of the formation had prevented unfortunate mistakes in recognition, and station-keeping had been excellent throughout. We then thought that the convoy had been wiped out at the cost of a small shell which burst in our tiller flat, wounding a leading stoker but doing no damage to the steering gear. No other ship had been touched, and the delay between closing up at action stations and opening fire on the enemy had been far less than in any exercise in which I had ever taken part!

The weather was again kind to us on the return passage, and we arrived without incident to find the signal 'Well done' flying from the mast-head of the Fleet Flagship, which was lying at anchor.

The result of the expedition had been most satisfactory. In fact, only two ships out of four were sunk, but even then it made a world of difference to the morale of us all. We felt that we were doing something for a living, and the ship became a much more cheerful place.

By September 1940 the most critical period of the invasion season was on, and we left Scapa, which was too far away from the Narrow Seas to be any good to us, for Rosyth. The change was welcome because, although there was little leave given, our boiler-cleaning periods at last were spent near civilization.

We saw a good deal of Coastal Command air crews on board at that time, and established a firm *entente* — which was, I fear, not general, for the many misunderstandings between the Navy and Coastal Command took some years of war to remove. I had one interesting flight to the Norwegian coast and back, on the last lap of which we were fired at, most inaccurately, by the escort of one of our convoys. As a result I had a deal of trouble in keeping my end up in the R.A.F. mess! The flight was entirely blank, but it was fun to have a look at that side of the North Sea again.

As a result of my visits to airfields, I was becoming the acknowledged expert on aircraft recognition on board. Naturally, I took every chance to further this fiction, and soon found the secret of the art. 'Say something quickly, and stick to it' was my motto, and I was seldom bowled out because aircraft, friendly or otherwise, used to keep well clear.

The Firth is an excellent exercise area, and Captain D took us out to sea most days of the week to try out the problems of attacking invasion convoys.

The flotilla also spent much time practising torpedo attacks on a single capital ship whose speed, it was assumed, had been reduced by air attack; and, although I left the ship before the plans bore fruit, Captain D must have blessed his forethought at the moment when the flotilla spread out to attack the *Bismarck* — an attack which helped to seal her fate.

As winter drew near it became certain that Hitler had missed his chance, and the flotilla returned regretfully to the cold bleakness of Scapa Flow. Life was drab then, but we at least started some serious seagoing again. At that stage of the war a report of a periscope by a zealous coast watcher in Iceland would send a division of destroyers hurtling off to spend a maddening few days chasing phantom contacts; while a friendly armed trawler with one gun forrard, which was reported as the *Lutzow*, brought the whole fleet to sea.

These scares, together with occasional trips screening the minelaying squadron who were completing an enormous barrage in the far north, were our only excitements, although we escorted one Atlantic troop convoy without incident. The trips with the minelayers were no picnic. The weather was invariably wicked, and these large ships and their battle-cruiser escort did not like to reduce speed for mere destroyers.

It was cold and wet on board, and very dangerous on the upper deck in bad weather. One black morning, when a boat on the upper deck abreast the foremast funnel was being resecured, we lost two men over the side, and a third was missing until he was discovered in the tiller flat, right aft, where he had been washed by the same sea which swept the other two overboard. I went over the side with the other three, but I was lucky enough to be washed back through the midships guardrails by the next wave, being picked up by the Captain of the Pom Pom who jumped down very quickly. I was shocked and badly bruised but had nothing broken, and I went straight up to the bridge to report to Captain D, who issued a monumental reprimand for leaving the ship without permission! Then I went down to the Engine Room Artificers' mess, which was just below the bridge, and more or less collapsed. The doctor was aft and could not get forrard owing to the weather, but an ordinary seaman who had been a medical student before joining the navy helped me to get over the after effects of shock. The E.R.A.s were most hospitable and looked after me very well, but it was a horrible experience and I spent a week in the hospital ship at Scapa afterwards and missed the next trip. One of the men who had been lost was the Chief Bosun's Mate, a splendid petty officer who had been with the ship since building, and there was much sadness aboard.

Once over the side, there was little chance. The water was icy cold, and it took time to turn the ship in the dangerous seas. These large destroyers did not ride over the waves, but seemed to dip the lee gunwale right under when they rolled. The force of the sea was unbelievable. Heavy steel lockers would be torn from the deck and lifted neatly over the guard rails; no one and nothing was safe on the upper deck. Weather damage was responsible for many destroyers being out of action unnecessarily. We got a corrugated bottom through failing to reduce speed quickly enough when escorting the battlecruisers, and leaks in the reserve feed tank developed, putting us in dock at Scapa for a quick repair.

Relieving the watch was a hazardous affair. The journey from the wardroom to the bridge was, especially at night, a terrifying ordeal. First, we climbed down into the gearing room, then up and over a bulk-head and down into the engine room, and finally there was about thirty yards of upper deck to be negotiated. There we crouched on the windward side, awaiting our chance to dash for the bridge ladder. We would arrive on watch wet through with a combination of sweat and salt water, which did not improve the next four hours.

Once or twice, it was too rough to allow anyone on the upper deck, so a select party of officers who happened to be forrard lived and slept for three days in the Engine Room Artificers' mess near the bridge, under the hospitable direction of the Chief E.R.A. The other E.R.A.s used to use our cabins aft, which were near the engine room.

But we were better off than other ships, which had no passage below the upper deck, and where men had to brave the whole passage without protection. Despite this, one man chose to ignore the order to use the engine-room route, and was never seen again.

The mess decks were indescribable in bad weather. Nothing the shipwrights of the depot ship could do would make the ammunition hatches around the forrard guns watertight, and the sailors' lockers used to wash about in the water, wetting their kits and making life a misery.

So passed the first part of the winter. Owing to a long trip off Iceland coming at an awkward moment, Christmas Day, 1940, was celebrated six days late. It was a good day, marred only by my old friend Spiteri, the wardroom cook, who somehow succeeded in getting himself into a shocking condition. Christmas Day can be a worry to a First Lieutenant, but a concert on the mess decks in the evening was a roaring success; and the day was as well enjoyed as is possible away from home.

A few days later, we were sent to Southampton to have our corrugated bottom permanently straightened and to get a short refit. Immediately after arrival, I was appointed unexpectedly to a command and left the ship at once.

I was delighted to be getting my first command, for some of my contemporaries had theirs already and I felt that I was being left behind. The *Cossack*'s crew were a grand crowd and they had not let their success affect their sense of proportion. Owing to the Narvik battle and the *Altmark* affair, the ship had become a '*Daily Mirror*' ship, which is normally bad for all concerned. But I was getting rather irritable and bad-tempered; perhaps I had been a First Lieutenant too long and it was time for a change of atmosphere. The *Cossack* was to add more laurels to her fame, before she was sunk, tragically and with heavy loss, later in 1941.

4. FIRST COMMAND

I HAD to leave the *Cossack* in such a hurry that I did not even see my relief, let alone get an opportunity of turning over to him. The chief points of importance were jotted down on paper, but turning over the ship's 'canteen fund' was not so easy, for keeping accounts had never been my strong point. The problem was solved by leaving a blank cheque with the audit, and I left light-heartedly for Belfast, where my new ship was lying.

During the last eighteen months I had had little opportunity to practise the art of navigation, for a First Lieutenant of a destroyer has more to do with the routine of the ship and its men than with the details of her progress from place to place. So, in the train, I read feverishly through my manual of navigation; for the urgency of my summons to the *Sabre* made me visualize her waiting only for the new Captain to step on board, before she let go all wires and steamed out into the Atlantic! My fellow passengers were most inquisitive. Apparently they thought that every naval officer should be able to work out his star sights without a textbook. But I was so thrilled by the thought of my first command that nothing they could say worried me.

Eventually I reached the docks where the ship was lying. 'Are you sure that this is the right ship?' I asked the driver, for instead of the trim ship I had expected to find, we had stopped alongside a rusty, battered-looking hulk, covered with workmen, whose bridge was only half completed and which lacked a mast.

But it was the right ship; the Admiralty practical-joke department had gained another victory, and I might well have stayed a couple of days in the *Cossack* to turn over thoroughly to my unfortunate relief.

The *Sabre*, when she was at her best, was a beautiful ship with lovely lines. She was one of a large last-war programme; and her class had been renowned both for speed and looks. Now she had been fitted with a formidable depth-charge armament at the cost of a gun and the torpedo tubes, and had been converted into an escort destroyer, for which she was well suited in all respects except that of fuel endurance. She looked terrifyingly small for the Atlantic, having been designed for short dashes in the North Sea during the First World War; but we found her a grand sea boat — she was handy, quick to accelerate, and her low silhouette made her almost invisible at night.

The *Sabre* had already acquired a glorious history as a result of her work at Dunkirk, where she had run the record number of trips to and from the beaches. Recently she had been badly damaged in a brave attempt to rescue the crew of a Dutch ship which had run ashore on Tory Island on the nor'western coast of Ireland in a full gale. The *Sabre* went in so close that she was almost among the breakers; and one great wave swept her decks, flattening the bridge and taking with it all the upper-deck fittings. The Captain had been badly injured and was still in hospital, but his was the worst case and fortunately no one had been lost.

The accommodation, both forrard and aft, was very cramped compared to the fleet destroyer which I had just left, and the washing facilities were limited; but the sailors seemed to be a good crowd, with a gem of a Coxswain who had that precious gift of producing a happy and contented ship. A great deal depends on the Coxswain of a destroyer; he is the leader of the ship's company, and we were very lucky to have such a good one. As I was to find later, the worse the weather and the filthier the conditions on the mess decks, the cheerier the sailors became. They were never depressed, and were the finest ship's company I have ever met.

Half the ship's company were on leave when I arrived, which was fortunate because, owing to the work in progress, living conditions were even worse than usual. There were workmen everywhere and the hammering of rivets continued day and night. To add to the discomfort there was snow on the ground, the ship's electric voltage was different from that of the mains ashore, power for heating was non-existent and the ship was bitterly cold. In fact, life was just about as grim as it can be in a ship in dockyard hands in winter.

The work went on surprisingly well, however, and in a fortnight the ship was ready for a day's trials in the Lough. This interval had been invaluable for me, for I was able to get to know the ship thoroughly, to brush up my sextant sights and to study the problems of ocean convoy work, which were all new to me.

The day when a Captain stands on the bridge of his first command and takes her to sea is a memorable one in his life. This time, we avoided a bump by a few feet when turning the ship in the narrow basin, and managed successfully to reach the exercise area. Everything on board was tried out, the engines were given a short run at full power, the guns were fired, the depth-charges released, the whaler lowered and sent for an imaginary man overboard, and the signal and wireless departments given many exercises to carry out. All went well, luckily, despite an abortive attempt to run down the whaler, when manoeuvring to recover her. Fortunately our engines were of greater power compared to our tonnage than in any other class of destroyer, and the boat's crew were just kicking off their sea boots, preparatory to a cold swim, when the 'full speed astern' took effect.

That night we sailed for Londonderry, which was our base. We arrived at dawn and proceeded up the long, twisting river, where, after a nerve-racking few minutes, I succeeded in getting alongside the oiler. This vessel was moored across the stream in the narrowest part of the river, and to approach her in any state of the tide except slack water was almost suicidal. Thank God, she was shifted soon afterwards to a berth alongside, for there would have been few escorts left undamaged if she had remained there much longer.

The passage up river was made under the guidance of an aged and garrulous Irish pilot with a long white moustache and a taste for whisky. He appeared to be half blind, and in addition nothing would budge him from the centre of the narrow channel, despite the heavy passing traffic. The experience was so alarming that I determined to learn my way about the river as soon as possible in order to undertake the trip without help, and I never took a pilot again.

We now met the other ships in the group, which was in the process of formation. It consisted of an assorted bunch of ancient destroyers, both British and American, of corvettes and of trawlers, all mostly new to the business; for at that time the fifty 'Four-Stackers', as the four-funnelled ex-American destroyers were called, and the new corvettes, were coming out from the yards in some numbers. The next two days were spent in planning and discussing the coming escort with our Leader, an officer of great destroyer experience with an irascible reputation; after which the group sailed in company. But not before I had celebrated my arrival by bumping the

Senior Officer's ship as she lay alongside the oiler! My alongside was made much too fast, the tide was tricky, but again 'full astern' saved the situation, and the only damage was some bent guard rails. The Senior Officer was not pleased, but he showed a surprising understanding of the affair, which was most comforting to my shaken confidence.

This sea going was an altogether different sort of life to that to which I had been accustomed. For one thing, speed had to be reduced to that of the trawlers; and for another, the signalmen were, of necessity, fewer and of a lower grade than those in a fleet flotilla; so that manoeuvring this unwieldy team was a lengthy process which must have been very irritating to our Leader.

The weather soon became bad, the ship was very wet and lively in a seaway, and tested the sea-keeping qualities of my insides, which just stood the strain.

On this trip the group was sailing direct to meet an eastbound convoy, so there were several quiet days before the escort proper started, though a corvette was detached in the middle watch one night to search for the survivors of a ship which had been torpedoed while sailing independently. With considerable skill she found the boats, after a day's search in bad visibility. But she had to return to harbour with the men, some of whom were in a poor way, so reducing the numbers of our escort by one.

After some hours of searching in heavy weather with visibility of under a mile, our convoy was found, and the group took up their stations, relieving the armed merchant cruiser which had been up to then the sole escort. The search would have been shortened considerably if the trawlers which first sighted the convoy had reported the fact at once, but these mistakes did happen at the start of the group system of convoy escort.

At this stage of the war, early in 1941, convoys did not get escorted right across the Atlantic but were instead given an armed merchant cruiser or battleship until they reached about twenty-five degrees west, where an escort group which had brought out a west-bound convoy met them and took them back to the U.K. Later in the year, the U.S. Navy took a hand and brought convoys as far as twenty-five west, where we took over. But 'through escort' right across the ocean did not come till much later and depended upon the presence of escort oilers in the convoys.

It is difficult unless one has seen it from the air to visualize the size and clumsiness of these vast convoys, which were at least six miles across and two miles deep when ships were in their proper station — which did not happen often. There were usually about a dozen columns, each containing four or five ships. The area was big and the perimeter which we had to protect was vast. Manoeuvring this mass of ships took time, and much time, too, was needed to get signals around the convoy, even by flags. Great forethought was required to get the necessary information signals out before dark each night.

Night was the anxious time for an escort, especially in bad weather. On a dark night it was by no means easy to keep in station; and it was not rare to find one or even two escorts adrift at dawn. In these circumstances the fear of enemy action receded into the background, and we had to concentrate on the purely domestic matters of keeping with the convoy and of avoiding weather damage. At the end of the first night we found ourselves in station, but during the rest of the next day the weather steadily grew worse, until a sou'westerly gale was blowing. As a result the rolling of the ship became so bad that the gyro compass broke and the asdics went out of action.

That night our station was on the port beam of the convoy, and two ships were chosen, both tankers (whose silhouettes are easy to identify), to whom we would cling during the night. I impressed the importance of not losing them on the Officer of the Watch and, after a final look round, went below to the chart house for a rest on the settee. I went up to the bridge two or three times during the night, always to get a good view of our two markers, and we were well satisfied with ourselves until, at first light, we realized to our horror that the two tankers were alone, and that there was no sign of the rest of the convoy whatever. The magnetic compass was not much use, and the divergence from the correct course during the night had not been noticed on the bridge — quite an easy thing to happen, yet rather shaking to have occur during the first 'driving' job.

A long worrying day and night followed. Visibility was still poor and no trace of the convoy could be found. Then, at dawn next day, we were able to see some stars, so fixing our position; and by comparison with the convoy's position, which had been received by wireless, we were able to rejoin with our charges before dark. I had spent most of the day signalling to the two tankers, encouraging them to greater speed, for I was worried lest we should not catch the main convoy. My threats were so effective that, when the convoy was finally sighted, we found ourselves fifteen miles ahead and had to turn back to join them, much to the annoyance of the Masters.

Our troubles were not over. During the day further disasters occurred. A wave had flooded a fuse-box on the bridge, putting out all lights there for the remainder of the passage and making it impossible to work the sounding machine except by hand, which was a lengthy business. In addition, the echo-sounding machine was put out of action. In fact, there was little on board which was working except the engines, which never failed in a full year's running.

A day or two later, before passing through the Minches (the channel between the Western Isles and the Scottish mainland) the convoy was formed into a narrow front, the *Sabre*'s job being to bring up the rear of the long lines. The Butt of Lewis, the northerly point of the islands, was sighted just before dark, and all went reasonably well before approaching the narrow passage between Shiant Island and Lewis.

Conditions were not easy because, to get a bearing of light, it was necessary to have a torch held over the compass bowl, which was swinging wildly; and chartwork, too, was difficult because there was no light in the chart table, which had been leaking badly, soaking the contents. Attempts to slide a parallel ruler over a wet chart in a heavy sea were not good for the temper.

When the Officer of the Watch lost sight of the last ship in the convoy, the situation quickly deteriorated. What made it worse was the sighting of a flashing light on the port side which, however hard we looked, we could not identify. A stop-watch was produced to time the intervals between flashes, and the chart was carefully scrutinized, but with no result. I decided to go on for a short time — then another light was sighted and again no trace of it could be found on the chart. By then I was quite lost; and after recovering from one more venture, which ended in our nearly running straight on to some menacing rocks, I stopped the ship and, with visions of losing my first command before my eyes, went down to the chart house to search all available Sailing Directions and Notices to Mariners for a clue to the mystery.

Suddenly, a shame-faced Navigator appeared with a piece of paper in his hand. 'This is it,' he said; 'I am afraid that I had forgotten to put these new light buoys on the chart!' From then on the way was clear, but the troubles of that shocking night were not over.

After safely negotiating Shiant Passage, I put my head in the chart table to check the new course. 'Green light close on the port bow,' was shouted by the Navigator, who was Officer of the Watch. By the time I had reached the compass he had ordered, 'Full ahead both,' and there was little to do but pray. Sparks flew out of the funnels as the engine room gave their best efforts. All I could do was to swing the stern over to starboard at the very last moment. The ringing of the telegraphs had brought Chief and Number One dashing up on deck, and they said afterwards that the other ship, a small coasting steamer, showing only dimmed bow lights, missed our stern by about two feet.

The Navigator had redeemed himself, for his quick action had saved the ship from the certainty of being rammed amidships. He had done the only thing possible and the engine room had responded nobly. This narrow passage should have been for 'one-way traffic' only, and in the misty weather the coaster was asking for trouble. There had been no time to feel frightened during the incident, but after it was over, my knees suddenly became weak. It was like the aftermath of an escape from a car crash, only far worse.

There were no more worries that night, and at daylight, being now well under the lee of the Hebrides, we were able to increase speed to catch the convoy, which was sighted about noon. By then they were off Barra Head and meeting the full force of the gale again. Some ships were hove to, the remainder were scattered, so that the escorts spent an unpleasant afternoon bumping around, trying to sort them out into sections according to their destinations.

In those early days the merchantmen were not so good at signalling, nor did they know the routine of convoy work as well as they were to later. Before dark, the *Sabre* was told off to escort the Clyde section of three ships as far as Greenock. The acting Commodore was a Norwegian tanker, to whom we made clear what was to happen, and exactly how and when she should lead the way from the main convoy. But it was not so easy with the other two ships, who would not or could not answer our signals, so I expected trouble when the time came to detach.

The chaos was worse than I thought possible. As the Norwegian turned off up the Firth, a heavy rain squall blotted out everything in sight. When it had cleared, a few minutes later, there were no signs of the other two ships; nor of the buoys, which marked the channel through the minefields. There followed a frantic search, which had so to be arranged that we also kept in touch with our acting Commodore. It was not a very safe performance. The night was dark and ships were not burning their navigation lights; but after some frightening moments, one more ship was found, a flashing light was sighted; and it was decided to concentrate on guiding our two 'birds in the hand' safely up the channel.

At dawn I went back to look for the missing ship, searching the Firth most thoroughly. There was no sign of her, and we did not sight her again. Feeling extremely guilty, I returned to base at best speed, with visions of courts of inquiry and other disasters; but on arrival, I found that our lost charge was perfectly safe and had decided to remain with the main convoy and to go on to Liverpool.

So ended my first escort in Command. It had been free from enemy interference and no headlines would flood the newspapers with our exploits; but perhaps it had not been quite so simple as the report, 'Convoy Number — arrived safely', suggests.

5. SECOND CONVOY

THE period in harbour after my first convoy in the *Sabre* was a busy one. It was necessary to impress firmly on those responsible on board the fact that the defects which had made the ship almost useless for several days during the last trip could not be tolerated, and that hard work on maintenance would soon prove them to be unnecessary.

There were many harbour drills to be carried out, and much to be discussed at the conference table.

Peter Scott, the wild-fowl artist, who was serving in the escort force, had produced a most effective camouflage, which we copied; so that two complete days were spent in applying the various tones which the scheme included. The final answer was a weird sight, but the result was excellent — almost too much so, because the first victims of the scheme were not the U-boats, but the ships concerned, which, being practically invisible on a dark night, were on more than one occasion run into by their friends.

After this, we sailed for our next convoy, which was outward bound for the Middle East. The passage was quiet at first except for the weather, which produced its usual gale, but during one night a ship in convoy, which was loaded with railway engines for Turkey, was in collision with one of the ships in the next column. She was hit in the engine room, which flooded, and she had to stop at once. Another destroyer, the *Scimitar*, was told off to stand by her. Next day they succeeded in getting her in tow after great efforts, but after another night of heavy weather, her bulk-heads gave way and she foundered. She went down so fast that only quick action by the seaman standing by aft in the *Scimitar*, who knocked off the towing slip, averted a dangerous situation.

One forenoon, about three days out, the *Sabre* was ordered to close the Senior Officer who was ahead of the convoy. His lamp started to flash as soon as we were in sight of him, and orders to search for and to escort an independently homeward-bound tanker, which had been bombed and damaged by Focke-Wulfs, quickly followed.

The position given was not far from the convoy, and we expected to meet her shortly. But she did not prove easy to find, for rain squalls made the visibility patchy. Happily a passing Sunderland flying-boat reported sighting a ship which he said was 'abandoned', and we went off in the direction given. The aircraft's estimated position was by no means accurate, and we would have missed her altogether had it not been for the starboard lookout, a Royal Naval Reserve fisherman from the Hebrides, who spotted her through the blinding rain.

We steered for the tanker at once, closing as near as I dared, and soon found out that she was a Dutchman who had been both bombed and attacked with cannon shell. The bombs had near-missed, putting one engine out of action, but the worst damage was to the bridge — it was riddled with shell-holes. Some officers and men had been killed, a small fire started and the compass hit and smashed, with the result that, although they could make a good ten knots, the ship could not be steered on course.

There were several wounded who required medical attention, but the weather made boat work too dangerous to attempt to transfer the doctor. He was furious. A red-headed native of the Western Isles, he had spent his youth in small boats and was keen to have a try. But the risk was too great.

After a short discussion about speed and other details, the tanker set off again, with the *Sabre* zig-zagging ahead to give her protection against possible submarine attack. The plan had been that the tanker should follow the mean line of our zigs, but it soon became clear that the scheme was quite impracticable. She went careering around and the quartermasters had evidently been set an impossible task. So we steered a steady course with the tanker following astern, not nearly such a safe proceeding, but the only one which would get us back to harbour before our fuel ran out.

The rest of her journey was a quiet one. Her remaining officers were most cheerful and the signalling excellent, so we had no troubles of any description. After a day's repairs the damaged engine was made good, enabling her to increase speed. The wind veered to a direction abaft the beam, and we were soon steaming up the Clyde, where a hospital boat was waiting to take the wounded ashore for treatment.

As soon as the Naval Control Service had taken over the tanker, we signalled 'Good-bye' and with our ensign dipped in honour of the dead steamed away at high speed to top up with fuel at Moville in the Foyle, thence rejoining the group as soon as possible. The tanker had saved over four-fifths of her valuable cargo, but our job was not finished. There were more ships to be brought in.

In order to save a few minutes I went through Rathlin Sound, the passage between the island and the Irish mainland, through which a five-knot tide was roaring — we flashed past Rue Point at about thirty knots. It was a beautiful scene; there was a 'race' off the point, while on the port hand towered the sheer, black and rocky cliffs of Fair Head, probably the highest in our Islands.

Before long the ship was alongside the oiler, and after a quick 'top up' we were steaming off at twenty knots. The Chief was a wizard at quick refuelling. He would get three hoses in board, two of which were lowered into the manholes of open oil-tanks and the other connected to the filling main, and we filled up in a remarkably short time. Once we were caught with three hoses in, when a sudden change of wind made a quick get-away from the oiler vital — but that is another story.

Intercepted signals had told us that the homeward-bound convoy, which our group had met by then, had suffered heavy losses. They had been sighted not long after leaving Gibraltar, the spies at Algeciras, across the bay, having made certain that the movement was known in Berlin, and subsequently had been attacked both by submarines and by Focke-Wulfs for several days. Serious casualties had been caused. The Commodore's ship had been torpedoed — the Commodore being picked up by an escort — and the Master of another ship was acting as Commodore of the convoy. They had still some distance to go before they were out of the danger zone, so it was up to us to move fast.

Luckily, the weather was perfect, we made a good speed, and, what was equally important, I was able to get plenty of sights, so ensuring that we should not waste time in finding them.

The meeting was rather spectacular because we picked up their smoke, at a distance of over twenty miles dead ahead. The time was later in the afternoon than I had expected but, owing to bomb damage to some ships, the convoy was not making its normal speed and was astern of its scheduled position. This was my first opportunity to show my unassisted skill with a sextant, for previously there had always been another ship present with whom positions could be exchanged. The thrill of this sighting, exactly where expected, filled me with confidence.

At dusk the *Sabre* took station on the port quarter of the convoy, and although there were one or two alarms, each a 'Non-Sub' due to whales or other fish, a quiet night was spent. The escort was now stronger, but before our group had joined it had been desperately weak because the destroyers, owing to lack of fuel, had been forced to return to Gibraltar.

Next morning the weather deteriorated and there was low cloud about. The hands were just turning to after breakfast, when there was a shout from the starboard lookout, 'Aircraft green three O!' The next thing I saw was a flash and a column of water in the convoy, followed by white smoke rising from a large ship in one of the centre columns. Then the aircraft flew across our bows, about a mile ahead, and was out of range before we had time to open fire.

A Focke-Wulf bomber had made a skilful approach out of low cloud, and had swooped down at mast-head height from the starboard bow of the convoy, taking both ships and escorts completely by surprise. We had no radar, and no warning was possible. He dropped two bombs, the first hit the foc'sle of one ship, bouncing off and exploding in the water without damage; but the other burst in a large meat ship, the finest ship of the convoy. The bomb went off close to her engine room, starting a large fire, and she soon had to stop, while a corvette stood by ready to take off the crew.

The last we saw of her was a blazing wreck on the horizon astern. She sank not long afterwards and, although the *Alisma* was able to pick up most of her survivors, she had had many casualties.

In the meantime the enemy was flying around watching the damage, and the best we could do was to fire an occasional round from the four-inch gun to prevent him getting too close. After about half an hour, having presumably counted the ships in convoy and reported our exact position, course and speed, he flew off back to France.

Although we expected the worst, for some reason unknown no further attacks, either by U-boat or aircraft, developed that day or the following night. All ships were keeping an especially sharp look-out, and the convoy must have spent an anxious night after an already protracted ordeal.

Next day was fine again. No Focke-Wulfs had appeared by noon, and after my midday meal I settled down on the settee in the chart house, which was also my sea cabin, to make up some missing sleep. A few minutes later the Yeoman of Signals came down with a signal from the Senior Officer, 'Number twenty-two has broken down, stand by her'; so I went up to the bridge cursing, and altered course to close the ship concerned — a Danish tramp steamer of a well-known firm, the Maersk Line. We closed her to carry out a long conversation, conducted by loud-hailer and answered by megaphone, on the subject of her repair. The loud-hailer is an excellent instrument for shouting advice or abuse to a ship, or for getting the answer 'Yes' or 'No' to questions; but it is not much help when the situation demands detailed replies.

The *Sally Maersk* was homeward bound in ballast from Gibraltar for much needed repairs in the United Kingdom. She had made a daring escape in the Straits of Gibraltar from a Vichy French convoy from Dakar and had offered her services to the Allies. Three days before we met her she had been near-missed by a bomb and her diesel engines, despite hard work by the engineers, had now failed, and the Master estimated that at least twelve hours would be required before they could be started again.

He was in a poor way, because two of his three deck officers had been wounded by cannon shells, and he had also had casualties among the crew. After some discussion we decided to try to tow her, for it was not healthy to be stopped in midocean at such a time, and the nearer we got to home the better we would be. The weather was good and, being very light in the water, she should tow with reasonable ease.

Now was the chance for which we had been waiting — a chance to show that many exercises had not been carried out in vain. I succeeded in making a good approach, and stopped the ship with the stern almost directly under the overhang of the *Sally Maersk*'s bow. A line was lowered, our wire was secured to it and the end hauled upwards.

Then followed a slight delay while a shackle was found which would join our wire to their cable. With the help of the Master, who was on the foc'sle head, supervising the work, this was managed; and the next thing to do was to persuade him to veer some of his cable into the water to act as a 'spring' when the weight came on the tow. This was the most difficult part of all because he said that his winch was defective, and that he would never be able to heave in the cable again. But after much argument he agreed — for it would have been madness to attempt to tow a 5,000-ton ship with a four-and-a-half-inch wire, unless there was some sort of spring in the tow.

The delicate operation of taking the strain of the tow and getting under way followed. To start off too fast meant that the wire must part, while always at the back of the mind was the thought of the sitting target we presented to a U-boat.

It was a very different matter trying to tow a ship of this size to exercising with a 1,000-ton destroyer. To add to the difficulty, during the time in which the towing wire had been passed, the *Sally Maersk* had drifted to leeward and our bow had swung off its course; so some tricky turning at rest was required before we could point in the right direction. It is never pleasant to move the engines with a large wire dangling directly over the screws, but eventually all was ready, and very gingerly the engines were put to dead slow ahead.

Presumably to relieve the tension while the *Sabre* was turning, two dogs put up a remarkable turn on the fore hatch of the Dane — an exhibition which was much appreciated by the ship's company, but which seriously distracted the bridge team from attention to the job in hand.

There was one awkward moment when, for a second, the bight of the towing line just lifted out of the water as the strain came on. But nothing parted, thanks to the weight of the cable, and soon we were on the right course, making good about five knots.

The tow went smoothly throughout the night and for most of the next day, and we were patting ourselves on the back for our good seamanship when BANG! the wire parted! It had gone at the splice, just outside our guard rails. Simultaneously, a signal came from the *Sally Maersk* to say that her engines were working again!

We swore that she started them by letting in the clutch and using the revolutions of the screw to turn over the engine, so putting an extra strain on the tow and causing it to part. She denied the charge hotly; but, whatever the answer, there was no doubt that she had four shackles of her cable and 124 fathoms of our wire hanging from the foc'sle with no power available to recover it. The only solution was the drastic remedy of slipping the whole issue. This was done and she proceeded on her way, complaining bitterly about the bill which the owners would have to face after the war!

When we left her off the Clyde we were well satisfied with the results of our labours. It had been a busy ten days; we felt we had done better this time, and, to crown our satisfaction, no awkward questions were asked about the loss of that four-and-a-half-inch wire.

6. MORE GALES

THE summer of 1941 passed quickly but quietly for the *Sabre*'s ship's company. Despite a fair supply of U-boats, which were well dotted about the Atlantic, our convoys seemed to be lucky, and we saw no submarines nor lost a ship. We had an anxious few moments when the *Bismarck*, with the Home Fleet in hot pursuit, passed fifty miles astern of our convoy, which was very lightly protected. Having no torpedo tubes left, we had often discussed what to do under these circumstances and had decided that a dummy torpedo attack followed by an attempt to drop depth-charges close ahead of her would be the only possible answer. So we rigged an oil drum, secured by a slip on the guard rails where the torpedo tubes had been, with a pipe from the auxiliary steam line. The idea was that when the time to 'fire' came, we would turn, let go the drum so that its splash simulated the torpedo hitting the water, and give a puff of steam to represent smoke from the charge. This was simple compared with shaving the bows of the *Bismarck* to drop depth-charges set to explode close under her bottom, but we were full of confidence of success if not survival. It was just as well that we did not have to try it out in earnest! But that was the only real excitement.

We also had the great pleasure of taking our Senior Officer, who was Escort Commander, in tow and hauling him some hundred miles towards Iceland. He was in an old Vee-class destroyer which developed condenser trouble, and, helped by good weather, we had no trouble in towing at quite a high speed.

The ship was kept very busy. We never missed a trip and the periods in harbour were few. By then the sailors had been shaped into a competent team who were very keen to show what the ship could do. Despite her age, she was running splendidly, and the engines were literally as good as new. The hull, however, was beginning to feel its years — cracks were appearing here and there, and we were seriously menaced by that distressing complaint, 'Water in the oil fuel'. The usual symptom of this malady was a cloud of white smoke pouring out of the funnels, and on one occasion there was so much water in the tanks that both furnaces were put completely out for a short time, while we lay stopped and useless.

In addition, oil fuel leaks proved a serious embarrassment owing to the number of times that keen-eyed planes would report 'suspicious oil tracks' in the wake of the convoy, and the airmen had hurt feelings if we took no notice of their reports. Frequent short dockings kept us running, however, and we were in good trim for the winter season.

We were lucky in our Chief, who was a Commissioned Engineer, and also in our 'Senior', who was a Chief E.R.A. of great experience who later became an officer. The Chief ended his long and distinguished service as an Engineer Commander, and well he deserved it.

The ship's company liked our base because the *Sabre* had been one of the first arrivals there and they had many friends ashore. In particular, the Coxswain and one of the petty officers had made great friends with some farmers near by. The Coxswain had started his shooting in river gunboats in China, while his companion, although the ship was too small to carry such a grand personage, had earned the honorary title of 'Gunner's Mate' aboard, and was in charge of our four-inch gun. Both owned shot-guns, and they got some good rough shooting during our spells in harbour. Several times I was lucky enough to go out with them. We had great sport the first time with hares, pigeons and a few partridges. The second day, too, with a more ambitious plan to seek out the woodcock, was good value in spite of the continuous rain, which was not allowed to interfere with the fun. Both men were useful shots and also were thoroughly safe with their guns. But the Coxswain's 'piece' put the fear of God into me. I kept well clear whenever he was about to discharge the weapon, for it was an ancient hammer gun, with one barrel lacking six inches as a result of a previous burst — it was only a matter of time before the other barrel followed suit. It was also possible to get an occasional day's hunting from Derry with the Strabane Harriers, and I used to go out whenever possible.

One day resulted in a close shave in missing my ship on sailing — a most serious offence. It came about as follows. I had the bad luck to fall off my horse and failed to catch the brute again. 'There I was,' as the pilots used to say, 'upside down and stranded in the Free State miles from anywhere and the ship due to sail at four o'clock.' By a combination of trudging, a donkey and a horse and cart, I just made it, and dashed up the brow to be greeted acidly by the Group Commander whose ship was out of action and who was taking passage with me. I ran up to the bridge, put on a raincoat to hide my hunting rig, and took the ship down the river to the oiler, where I was able to change into uniform.

I also got some shooting at Lough Erne, the local flying-boat base, where, with the aid of some friends in the R.U.C., I was shown some fine places for duck. Much credit was earned, too, for doing some flying in the Sunderlands and Catalinas based there, and what with the shooting and the excellent mess at

Castle Archdale, it was a splendid way to spend a boiler-cleaning leave.

After this particular interval in harbour, as was always the routine, the group carried out various exercises before finally sailing for the convoy. The *Sabre* was unlucky enough to be detailed to take out a well-known journalist to watch these exercises. He was personally a charming man, but he wrote a daily column in a popular newspaper, and we were terrified of what might appear!

One impromptu turn was put up by the whaler's crew, who succeeded in capsizing their boat when about to exercise boarding a submarine. The order to 'slip' the boat was given, correctly, while the ship was still going ahead at about eight knots, but the after fall failed to release, and the bows dived under the water. This mishap amused the crew of the submarine no end — massed in the conning tower to repel boarders, they were able to exercise their best 'German' with ingenious gibes at the swimming men.

It took a great deal of persuasion before our guest promised to forget this black affair, but luckily he had been so impressed by the language of the Captain of the destroyer in which he had taken passage from Liverpool that he hardly noticed us, and could talk of little else but his recent experiences.

Asdic conditions off Londonderry could be very bad in some states of wind and tide, and this was one of them. I regret to say that during the A/S exercise we even lost sight of the 'buffs' which the submarine towed on the surface to show her position, and we lost her completely. For some reason she did not surface at her correct time, and I got very worried about her safety. Fortunately she popped up miles away soon after, but I fear that Mr. Collie Knox can have had but a poor regard for our skill.

On another trip we took the Catholic Chaplain from the base to sea in order that he could get an idea of what his flock had to endure. He was a splendid man who had collected an M.C. when he was Chaplain to the Australian Army in the First World War. He was widely travelled, well educated and tolerant, and a very different type to the normal run of priests in County Londonderry. He was later given a naval commission and did very well in the Mediterranean, and I was always glad that I had been able to give him his first taste of a warship at sea. Father Devine got on well with everyone on board, including the Orangemen of whom we had one or two, and I shall never forget the Coxswain coming on to the bridge one Sunday morning and saying that the messdeck would like a non-denominational service, and would Father Devine take it! He did. He acquired a great affection for the sailors and would never allow his flock to go to sea unshriven, lest they be lost that trip. I often remember seeing him leaning against the sentry box on the jetty opposite a ship due to sail shortly, confessing the sentry at his post! My wife and I are proud to say that he married us later in the war.

After the exercises which Mr. Knox had watched were over, the group topped up with fuel, dropped Mr. Knox and sailed for the next convoy, which was bound for Canada. Promptly we met our usual 'Oversay' weather, which seemed always to appear when we were due at this rendezvous. This 'Oversay' mixture usually included rain and heavy seas and always low visibility, a fact which made the meeting of the sections as they joined up from the main unloading ports a most hazardous affair. Invariably one section would be early and another late, so that some ships had to be turned round and others whipped up, in an effort to get the whole convoy in fair order before dark. This time matters were further complicated by the unexpected appearance of one of the newly constructed Catapult ships, which carried a fighter on the foc'sle. This machine was designed to be flown off to deal with the Focke-Wulfs, which were then not only bombing convoys, but also shadowing and reporting their positions to the waiting U-boats.

The convoy had not been warned of the sailing of this ship, which was still on the secret list, so I spent an unpleasant couple of hours steaming up and down the columns, warning the ships not to fire at the Hurricane after it had been shot off. This warning was most necessary because the flash and smoke of the Catapult resembled a bomb hit, and already there had been some unfortunate incidents in convoy. The loud-hailer batteries were almost finished, and my voice was extremely hoarse by the time we had completed the round of all ships.

The outward passage was uneventful. But in these days of efficient radar and radio navigational aids it is easy to forget the difficulties in those times, when the visibility in winter was usually poor. We would spread the ships at visibility distance apart, sometimes a little more, and steam down the estimated track of the convoy. Radio silence was strictly enforced, and we never knew whether the convoy would be late or early or, indeed, on its right track either. Astronomical navigation was often impossible for long periods as one could see neither sun nor stars, and dead reckoning was difficult. The thrill of a 'Meet' after the suspense of the search was very real.

At this stage in the Atlantic struggle, the lack of ships made trans-ocean escort impossible. 'Mid-ocean' groups had not yet been formed, so, reluctantly, we had to abandon our convoy somewhere south-west of Iceland in order to fuel at Reykjavik before the homeward-bound trip with the next convoy. A few hours after leaving them, an SOS was received from our late

Commodore. The convoy had been attacked, three ships had been torpedoed, and help was urgently needed. The U-boats must have waited for our departure and then attacked, secure in the knowledge that the convoy was undefended.

We rushed back at full speed, soon sighting two ships lying helpless, one well down by the stern. Of the third there was no sign whatever — an old tramp-steamer, she had been hit by two torpedoes and had sunk like a stone. We were lucky to find two men, the only survivors, on a raft which had floated off her as she went down.

Boats were scattered over the water near the other two, who had, I am afraid, abandoned ship too soon. It is difficult to blame them; but secret books had been left on board both ships, one of which, loaded with timber, must take a long time to sink. So, while another destroyer steamed around to protect us, the *Sabre* towed the boats back to their ships and persuaded two rather reluctant parties to get back aboard again.

At times of tragedy it is often the comic scenes which impress the mind. The Commodore was in one boat. An elderly man, he had on only a greatcoat over his pyjamas, and he had left his false teeth on board — facts which seriously hampered both his freedom of speech and his dignity.

His ship sank shortly afterwards, fortunately without further casualties, and it was found impossible to steam the timber ship, which, despite her submerged stern, was capable of remaining afloat for weeks.

All survivors were transferred to the rescue ship, and the Senior Officer decided to sink the cripple, since no tug was available and no escort could be spared to tow. He must have regretted this decision, however, because gunfire was quite ineffective for the job, and two torpedoes, I regret to say, missed. So one ship was left to sink her with depth-charges, and the group, already late and getting short of fuel, set off again for Iceland.

Iceland was a horrible place to 'make' if the weather was unfavourable. Soundings gave little warning of the vicinity of land, and the first intimation was liable to be the roar of the waves breaking against the high cliffs. But Reykjaynes Point was picked up successfully, and after negotiating the entrance to the fleet anchorage (another awkward proceeding in low visibility) the group was soon alongside the oiler.

It was most necessary to identify clearly the ship to the port signal station before approaching the entrance, for the army were notoriously quick on the trigger and the coast defence guns had more than once opened fire on carefree and overcasual escorts.

Normally we were allowed a full day in harbour there, but this time we were already behind schedule. These spells sometimes gave us a chance to see Reykjavik, where silk stockings were cheap and the black-out non-existent. But these were the only attractions, because the surrounding country was bare and desolate, and the manners of the inhabitants were correct but hardly cordial.

After sailing, which occurred immediately fuelling was finished, the first thing to do was to find the rescue ship, which, escorted by the corvette *Dianella* who did not need to refuel, was 'marking time' some way to the south-west. These useful ships, who were well fitted to deal with survivors, used to transfer from the outward-bound convoy with the group. They did great work, their boat work, particularly, being magnificent.

While searching for them a signal was received saying that our convoy had met very bad weather, would be late at the rendezvous, and was badly scattered. Simultaneously an SOS was received from a ship of the same convoy, which had been torpedoed in a position far ahead of where the main body should have been. The victim was a whale-factory ship, which was still able to steam; and the corvette *Sunflower* was sent to her help. The rescue ship and her escort were left on their own, and the rest of the group was spread out in line abreast in order to find the incoming convoy, which must be given escort as soon as possible.

They were evidently bringing the bad weather with them for, as we approached the area, the visibility decreased and the wind got up rapidly.

The chapter of accidents which follows does not, I fear, 'reflect great credit on all concerned'. The convoy was eighty miles from its signalled position. The group, whose trawlers were never all they should have been at the art of station-keeping, got split up and thoroughly lost, and it was the rescue ship and her escort who were the first to find the main body! Our sister ship, the *Shikari*, had the bad luck to lose her funnel, which was knocked flat by an enormous wave, and she was forced to return to Iceland — which she succeeded in reaching after a hazardous passage with no aids to navigation whatever.

Again the comic side is the easiest to remember. The *Shikari*'s main aerials had been swept away by the sea, and she could transmit only by radio telephone. The telegraphist working the set, a Yorkshireman without a doubt, seemed only able to repeat the words 'Situation grave', with monotonous regularity, and refused to produce other details. We were practically hove-to ourselves and had not the first idea of where she was, anyhow; so there was nothing we could do about the matter except to laugh at the operator's broad accent and to hope for the best. Ever afterwards on the *Sabre*, if anyone so much as broke a plate aboard, the usual lower-deck profanity was replaced by a sorrowful 'Situation grave!'

That afternoon the ship was plugging slowly ahead into the easterly gale, when we met the whale-factory ship, escorted by the *Sunflower*, who had been lucky to find her so quickly. She was making good speed towards Iceland and appeared undamaged until, well past the beam, we could see an enormous hole in her side like the entrance to a railway tunnel. Fortunately she arrived safely with her valuable cargo, which, besides oil, included many aeroplanes.

This brighter incident was soon dimmed by another SOS; this time from a tanker, which had also 'romped' from the convoy, and had been torpedoed several hundred miles ahead. As a result, the convoy was diverted to the southward of the danger area, making it even more difficult to find. However, with the help of great luck and of a sort of sixth sense which we were rapidly acquiring, the *Sabre* found the convoy before dusk and, taking station ahead, relieved a grateful *Dianella* who had no asdics left as a result of the gale and who therefore was barely half effective.

It was a proud moment. We had 'beaten the group to it', and we were now acting as Senior Officer of the escort of this valuable convoy. I fear that any worries about the responsibility of protecting so many ships with one and a half escorts did not weigh very heavily upon us, owing to the thrill of sending off to all concerned the laconic signal, 'Met'.

After a most unpleasant night, during which great difficulty was found in keeping in touch, the next day was spent in homing the rest of the group to the convoy — a proceeding which gave us a great sense of superiority. By the day after that they were all in station, and with the help of aircraft from Coastal Command the stragglers had been rounded up and the convoy reformed. The weather improved suddenly at noon, and with the change came a most appropriate biblical signal from the Commodore.

Early in the middle watch that night, the Commodore flashed a signal, 'Have passed boat in water.' We investigated at once, and after a short search in pitch darkness we found a life-boat containing ten men. The sea was calm with a little swell and our men had little difficulty in lifting them inboard, as the boat rose up to the level of the gunwale.

Their story must be one of the luckiest of the war. The boat was the second life-boat from the 'romping' tanker. During the two days after the torpedoing, they had drifted aimlessly to the southward and, by an astonishing stroke of fortune, had so hit off the convoy that they had been nearly run down by the Commodore's ship, which led the centre column. Owing to the diversion of route, our track was over a hundred miles to the south of the position of attack. The Atlantic is vast, and it was indeed a miracle that they were saved.

The tanker had been loaded with benzoline which, spreading over the water, had caught fire. The boat and its occupants had been badly burnt, the Mate and one Chinese from the crew dying of shock. The other eight men were placed in the officers' cabins, and in the wardroom; and the doctor spent an anxious and busy time in tending their severe burns. The three remaining Chinese had been put in the wardroom, where two quietly lay on the settees and one squatted in a chair. Not a trace of emotion or suffering was ever allowed to be shown, not a complaint was uttered, and the only words which we heard from them were 'Thank you'. Happily, all eight survived.

Next day the *Sabre* was given permission to go ahead at best speed to land the injured men. We wasted no time, and it was not long before the ship was alongside a berth at Londonderry, to find a team of ambulances awaiting our arrival.

Again we had failed to meet the enemy, but again the passage had not been uneventful. This time we reaped a reward, for our last burst of speed got us in so early that we were able to spend one more day in harbour than the rest of the group.

Some time in the autumn of 1941, I cannot remember exactly when, we were sent to Belfast for a quick docking and the fitting of a radar set (called R.D.F. in those days). I had been asking for a set for some time and was delighted at the prospect, but it was not all plain sailing. The set had been designed for an aircraft and had a fixed mattress-type aerial on the foremast. One had to point the ship to get a bearing of an echo and to weave the ship continually in order to search. This was very awkward. The set was in the metric wave-band and owing to the poor discrimination was little good at picking up submarines, except in perfect weather. However it was invaluable for station keeping and for searching for surface ships, both at night and in poor visibility. The final snag was that only in the chart house was there room for the set itself. The chart house was also my sea cabin in which I had meals, washed (except in very fine weather when I used a bucket on 'A' gun deck) and slept. It was not much fun either for the radar operators or myself to have to share this small space, and great tolerance was required on both sides! However, it was an advantage to be able to see the radar screen without getting up from one's bunk.

I know now from the Doenitz memoirs that there were few U-boats at sea in the North Atlantic during the last months of 1941. The reasons for this state of affairs were many. The building programme, started on the outbreak of war, had not begun to affect the flow of new boats, and losses, which were heavy, were only just being replaced. Secondly, Hitler and the High Command kept ordering diversions from what Doenitz considered was the main aim of attacking the Atlantic life-line. Some boats were employed as weather reporters for the German Air Force, others were sent off to fight the Russians and others still to the Mediterranean to bolster the Italian Navy. In December 1941 Doenitz had only five boats available for Atlantic operations — which accounted for the quiet time we had then in the *Sabre*.

7. A NEW SHIP

AFTER fifty-three weeks continuous running, the *Sabre* went off to refit early in 1942. We had not spent more than eight consecutive days in harbour during all that time, and had logged over half of the year under way; so that both the ship and her company needed a rest.

My relief arrived almost at once, and, after some anxious moments over the Confidential Book muster — which was successfully completed only when a valuable document was unearthed from beneath the Sub's bunk — I packed up and left the ship for three weeks' leave.

It was a wrench to leave such a grand crowd. The first command is always an especial favourite; but now that convoys were escorted right across the Atlantic, her short fuel endurance was beginning to limit her usefulness. The ship's company had been a first-class team, and it was extremely disappointing that we had no U-boats to show for all the hard work and for the convoys helped safely to harbour. In particular, the 'S'-class destroyers had the biggest depth-charge armament of any ship in the navy and we much wanted to try it out in earnest, but it was not to be.

I do not think that anyone who has seen the mess decks of a small ship at sea in wartime can appreciate the conditions under which the sailor lived. He was either 'four hours on and four hours off' watch or, if enemy attack was unlikely, 'four hours on and eight hours off', as well as closing up at action stations regularly at dawn and dusk, and sometimes during the day and night, too. This meant that he spent well over one-third and often well over one-half the twenty-four hours on watch. When off watch he had to collect and sometimes prepare his meals, wash, keep the ship clean, and live his own life in what remained of the day. The mess decks were always wet in bad weather and the facilities for drying clothes inadequate. The sailor had also, if he was lucky enough to find a slinging billet, to sling and lash up his hammock every morning, which was an exhausting feat in bad weather. In the *Sabre* we ended up with a ship's company of about 120 men living in a ship built for between seventy and eighty, and they were packed very tight indeed. It was a remarkable feat of endurance to exist, to work and to remain cheerful in these conditions, but they did it, and they came up smiling at the end of every trip. It was the same in the small ships of the navy throughout the war. Most of them were more modern than the *Sabre*, but the corvettes, for instance, were far more lively in a seaway and were very tiring indeed in bad weather.

As for the officers, we had cabins, food produced for us, a wine bar, and someone to make one's bed and wash out one's underclothes from time to time. It was a very different life, though of course we had the responsibility, which perhaps is the worst strain of all.

But I do not think that enough tribute has been paid to the ordinary British sailor, both regular and 'hostilities only', for his guts and, although he would never own up to such a quality and would laugh bawdily at the suggestion, his genuine devotion to duty.

The chance to visit Ireland was too good to miss, so, having failed to catch the best train owing to the Sub's casual habits with confidential books, I cajoled my way into a returning cattle train and enjoyed an unconventional trip to Dublin in remarkable company. As I also found later, the sight of a pair of hunting boots slung over my suitcase was the sure pass to preferential treatment from any Irishman.

The ten days following made a wonderful break. Lights, no war, and the abundance of food were almost too good to be true. I did all the right things: sampling the well-known Meath drains; getting stuck on a bank in the Limerick country; and, as a contrast, seeing a Sean O'Casey play at the famed Abbey Theatre in Dublin.

There were no trains running, and the story of the bus journey between Dublin and Limerick would fill a book. Although it took over six hours, there was never a dull moment. The passengers included the most diverse types possible to imagine. In the front seat was a bishop with his wife, travelling back to his diocese in the west; and behind them was a large family with much luggage. That was the smug section. In the centre there were some farmers with their wives, a priest, and a couple of army officers in their green uniform; and in the rear, my companions included an amateur jockey off for the round of the point-to-points, a couple of obvious sailors on leave from the fleet, looking rather awkward in plain clothes, and a commercial traveller who, knowing every inch of the journey, constituted himself my guide and adviser. We were not smug in the back!

The bus stopped at twelve towns, and in twelve dingy bars we had at least one drink. By the Curragh, the back seats were all old friends; by Roscrea, songs were being sung and improbable tales related of the scarcity of foxes, of German parachutists, and of the coming race winners; by Nenagh, I fear, the Bishop's ears were turning red, and the general trend became ribald, to put it mildly; and at Limerick I had to swallow much black coffee before going on to meet my hosts.

Plans for a final grand wind up with the famous Duhallow and Scarteen packs had just been made, when a telegram arrived from the Admiralty. 'Report at Devonport forthwith,' it said. Having been caught so often before, I put a call through to London — no mean feat in wartime Ireland — and succeeded in getting through to the officer responsible. 'Is my journey really necessary?' I asked. 'Yes, old man,' came the reply, 'your new ship completes refit very shortly, and you must get to work straight away.'

With visions of catching a waiting aeroplane and being flown out to the Mediterranean, I caught the next bus to Dublin and was soon back in the *Sabre*, where I collected my uniform. There I found that my next ship was the *Wolverine*, a destroyer which was refitting; but, still with the magic word 'forthwith' in the forefront of the mind, I spared neither trouble nor expense to get myself and no less than eighteen pieces of baggage, including gunboots and golf clubs, down to Devon-port.

After a nightmare journey via Larne, Stranraer and London, I finally arrived with sixteen pieces and no gasmask, and hurried to report to Captain D.

'Hullo, I *am* pleased to see you, I did not expect you for another fortnight,' he greeted me. 'Your ship is nothing like ready yet; would you like to go on leave straight away or wait here a week?'

The practical-joke department had won again.

There was over a month to wait before the ship could be completed. Time passed reasonably quickly because there was much to do, both in the ship and with its crew, before she was ready for sea. The *Wolverine*, which had made history by putting in the bag the U-boat ace Gunther Prien and also sinking one other submarine, had paid off, and only a dozen of the old crew were left. We were able to give many officers and men special courses in various technical subjects, and Number One spent some considerable time 'lobbying' at the drafting office, where the allocation of men for the ship was arranged. This long wait also gave us time to get to know each other well. There were good opportunities for games, and some enthusiastic soccer resulted — in which the officers held their own, for I always insisted that we should provide the referee, who was trained to ignore our rough methods. I also had some hunting on Dartmoor.

One day in April 1942, well before our trials were due to start, I was on board watching some new gear being hoisted in, when a messenger came running up to say that Captain D wished to see me at once. The basin in which we were lying was only a couple of moments from Captain D's offices, and within five minutes I was back on board again, shouting for my cabin hand to be fetched immediately and starting to collect clothes.

The Captain of the *Brocklesby*, a Hunt-class destroyer due to sail in fifteen minutes' time, had gone sick unexpectedly; a temporary Captain was required and I was the only one available. I was soon on board her, and walked straight up on to the bridge. The First Lieutenant reported 'Ready for sea', and we slipped from the buoy and steamed out into Plymouth Sound. I knew the wardroom well, having been on board in harbour, so the officers were not strangers, but it was an odd feeling to be taking a ship to sea, on whose bridge I had never been before.

The week which followed was most interesting. It was my first experience of Channel convoys, of which I had read so much in the papers, and the problems involved were totally different to those to which I had been accustomed. Instead of U-boats and Focke-Wulfs, E-boats, mines and dive bombers were the most likely forms of attack; and, of course, the convoys were much smaller, both in number and in the size of the ships, than Ocean convoys. But we had a most efficient screen of fighters throughout, and the passage up Channel was quiet.

At the terminal port, Cowes, we had one night in harbour, and next day were off again with the return convoy. Before sailing, a signal was sent to the ship saying that the convoy conference would be held ashore at ten-thirty. Accordingly, as Senior Officer of the escort, I reported at the Naval Control Office at that time. On arrival I could see no signs of any Masters about, and was wondering whether the time had been correct, when the head man came in.

'Good morning,' he said. 'Are you the Senior Officer escort? Right, just follow me, will you,' and he led the way out to the Silver Anchor next door, where I found the lounge bar full of Masters and Captains of escorts. He must have noticed my surprise for he said, 'Oh, you're new to the game, are you? You see, these chaps have been doing the same run for two years now and they all know the rules backwards. We usually talk in here now.' So, after an illegal glass of ale, a quick meeting was held, with the Commodore of the convoy as the main speaker, and the barmaid, a fat, cheerful old thing who knew far more about coastal convoys than I did, ably presiding.

Afterwards we returned to our ships, setting off immediately on the westbound journey, which again was uneventful.

Before I left her, the ship had one more job. We went into the Atlantic for a short distance to meet and help escort up Channel a large Union Castle liner, which had been torpedoed some time previously. Then she had been full of troops, and the Master had had an anxious time getting her safely back to harbour because her stern rudders had been blown off, leaving only the propellers intact. Now, after temporary repairs, she was due to be docked and rebuilt. When we met her, she was making excellent speed, although her course was rather erratic, and she had left the tug which was supposed to be helping her to steer miles astern!

Again there was no excitement, and when we arrived at Devonport I returned to my own ship, after a pleasant breath of fresh air, most welcome after the smoky atmosphere of the dockyard.

Work had not gone as well as we had hoped because conditions at Devonport were bad and, in addition, female labour seemed a mixed blessing. Eventually we were ready to do our full-power trials — necessary because the ship had been given new boilers, which must be tried out at speed.

The trials were not a success. The day was a fine one, so that high speed would be possible although a low mist over the water made it a little risky. We had on board one or two dockyard officers to take records and observe results, and also we had invited a dentist from the naval barracks, who had never been to sea, to come for a day's outing. Everything seemed satisfactory on starting, and after exercising 'action stations' as we passed through the boom, the ship's company reverted to normal 'cruising stations', and the hands were piped to dinner.

About four minutes later the Yeoman of Signals reported 'Sound of aircraft on the port beam', and two single-engined planes appeared out of the mist about half a mile away, flying straight towards us. There was an anti-aircraft practice firing range at Breakwater Fort in that direction, so I made yet another contribution to the list of famous last words, and replied 'Friendly fighters'. As the words left my mouth, flashes of flame appeared from the wings of both planes, and machine-gun bullets whizzed about the ship in a most alarming manner. There was no time to do anything. The two Messerschmitts were approaching at about 400 knots and, 100 yards off the ship, they each dropped a bomb from mast-head height.

One bomb was aimed badly, missing astern; the other looked as if it would do the same, until it hit the water short of the ship. But then it produced a vicious break from the leg, bounced over the after gun, and landed in the water close to the starboard side of the engine room. It sank quickly and exploded at a depth of about fifty feet.

I can see that bomb now! It was turning slowly through the air, showing clearly the yellow bands around its black belly, and it seemed an eternity before it fell — just clear. The bridge oerlikons had been only able to get off a few rounds at the retiring planes, and did them no harm, but the bullets sufficed to prevent them coming in again.

The bomb must have weighed about 500 pounds, but fortunately it did surprisingly little damage. The engine room reported minor breaks to steam pipes, which would make it impossible to carry on with the trial, and the doctor reported that one man had been killed outright by a machine-gun bullet. I returned to the dockyard immediately.

On the way we passed the *Brocklesby* and another Hunt who had also been attacked — by four planes, whilst they were passing through the boom gate. Being still at action stations, they had opened fire at once and had knocked down two ME-109s and damaged another, without casualties or more serious damage than a few holes in the funnel. They were cock-a-hoop, especially the *Brocklesby*, where the Yeoman of Signals, who needed to have no knowledge of the gun, grabbed the port bridge oerlikon and, filling up the Hun with bullets in a masterly manner, had watched it dive into Cawsand Bay in flames.

The enemy had chosen their time well. It was the dinner hour ashore and afloat, the low haze made it impossible to see them until the last moment, and they had caught the defence by surprise. They made a good attack, and had it not been that these two Hunts had been at action stations, they might all have got clean away with it.

Our minor damage did not take long to repair, the next trial was more satisfactory, and within a week we were ready to sail for service. During this week, the ship's company had been very generous to the next of kin of their dead shipmate. He had been well liked both forrard and aft, and was married with a large family of young children; so a 'sale of effects' was held on board, at which his kit was offered to the ship's company. Although a large majority of the lower deck had been in the navy less than a year, they responded grandly to the example of the older men. Time and time again, pieces of clothing were bought for much more than they were worth, to be thrown back into the pool for yet another auction. The final sum well reflected on their spirit, and there is no more generous man in the world than the British sailor.

About then, in midsummer of 1942, I got my 'half stripe'. I was now a Lieutenant-Commander, which called for celebration, though the advancement was routine and depended solely on seniority.

The next job was to 'work up' our green crew, half of whom were serving in their first ship; so, immediately repairs had been completed, we sailed for our exercise area at Londonderry.

We did not reach it on time, however, for off Land's End we received a signal diverting us to Cardiff for our first operational job.

After a useful day at anchor in the Roads, where many exercises of every description were carried out, I went ashore to find out what our plans were to be. At the local naval offices, I was given orders to escort a cargo liner, which was due to join a secret convoy to the Clyde starting that afternoon. I thought I might go on board the ship on the way back to the *Wolverine* and make my number up on the Master, so I asked a loafer on the dock side where it was lying.

'Oh yes,' he replied, 'that's the ship that is sailing for Malta today,' and pointed to a fine-looking vessel across the basin.

This same ship was sunk a week later in the Mediterranean and her convoy also suffered heavy losses.

The weather was fine for our work-up and, helped by a good deal of local knowledge, we had a useful week's exercising, during which the ship began to look as if things might work properly in time. This period is one in which perpetual patience is required. There were few experienced officers or men aboard, and every mistake had to be made, sometimes twice, before Number One and I felt that it might not happen again.

At the end of the week we went up river to get Sunday in harbour and to have a spell from intensive training before the last week of the work-up started. After Church we were sauntering back on board, looking forward to a forenoon gin followed by an afternoon in the country, when a messenger on a bicycle arrived.

'Raise steam with all dispatch, further orders follow', the signal said and, with our prospects of rest shattered, we hurried back to the ship.

On board, preparation for sea was well under way, and within two hours we had slipped and were on our way down river, having left behind two men only, both of whom were on local leave. Two large ships in a convoy had been in collision some distance off the south-west of Ireland; our orders were to meet them and escort them back to harbour. Speed was essential because they had an escort of one corvette only, and the worst-damaged ship threatened to sink at short notice.

As the *Wolverine* rounded the headland which protects the entrance to the River Foyle from south-west gales, she began to pitch heavily, making it necessary to reduce speed to twenty knots. The sea was coming green over the bridge, which was wet and draughty, and many leaks in the deckhead were soon evident. By the time we had passed Tory Island and altered to the south-west, we were pushing straight into a moderate gale, and speed had to be reduced again. At this stage, a grinning Number One came up on the bridge to report that he had been around the mess decks, that the leaks left by the yard were many but not serious, and that only about a dozen seamen, almost all of them petty officers, were not lying 'flat out' on the mess tables, lockers, or deck! Also, despite countless warnings, the mess decks had not been properly secured for sea, and mess traps, boots, buckets and bodies were slithering from side to side. The place was a regular shambles.

It was just as well that the ship was not called upon to fight the Germans that night; the result would not have been a happy one, as many of the sailors would have preferred to die rather than move!

We got an accurate 'departure' from Eagle Island light and then concentrated on the problems of finding our ships. The Sub, who was navigator, was brand new, straight from his courses ashore. He had spent most of his time at sea as a midshipman shut up in a fire-control room, deep in the bowels of a battleship. No doubt he was invaluable there, but the result was that his experience with a sextant was limited to shooting a cardboard sun in a schoolroom, and to taking sights at anchor in Scapa Flow, where no horizon can be seen. So, for the first month or two, I used to take sights with him.

We knew the position, course and speed of our quarry, and it should have been a comparatively simple matter to find them, if only we could get a sight of the sun. After getting well clear of Ireland, the wind decreased and the sea went down, so that we were able to increase speed again, and the ship's company rapidly recovered their best form. About noon the sun appeared, and after a couple of attempts by the Sub, who found a cramped and bucking chart house quite a different place for working out sights to a classroom at the Navigation School, we got a Latitude.

I was worried about the chance of meeting them. In the run since leaving Eagle Island, there was room for a fairly large error in our dead reckoning, for I did not know the ship, nor how accurately her revolutions compared with the supposed speed. By the time a sight for Longitude could be got, we would have passed the estimated position of our quarry, so anything might happen.

It is usually the fellow with the greatest interest in the sighting who sees things first at sea. That is the reason the navigator sights lights before the look-outs. Sure enough, while anxiously scanning the horizon, I saw, very wide on the bow, a puff of smoke which disappeared at once. No one on the bridge believed me, but I altered course towards the bearing, and shortly there appeared the tall, thin funnel of one of the Harrison line, and I knew we had found them. It was a lucky meeting, and we might easily have missed them if we had not altered course.

On closing the *Crocus*, which was the only escort, we found out that the Harrison ship had a flooded fore peak and fore hold, and was badly down by the bows; and that the other ship had been rammed in the engine room, luckily a little above the water line. Both were going well, but both would be in a bad way if the weather got any worse. The sooner they got in, therefore, the better would be their chances of safety.

Next day our little convoy passed straight through a fleet of Spanish trawlers fishing on the Sole bank. We suspected that they were used by the Germans for reporting shipping, but it was out of the question to board each one of them. I told the *Crocus* to board and search one, however, in order to discourage any spying. A corvette's boat work is liable to get a little rusty, and I do not know which was most shaken by this episode, the *Crocus* or the trawler. But it was well managed and, although neither spies nor wireless gear were found, a tin of baccy produced enough fish to feed the ship for weeks.

That afternoon a flying-boat from Plymouth arrived to escort us. By some chance, the Australian crew were old friends from 10 Squadron with whom I had spent one long Bay patrol; so we both exercised our 'visual' with some rude signals.

Next morning I fully expected an attack by bombers from the bases on the French coast, for it seemed probable that one of the trawlers had reported us; but nothing happened. A fighter escort arrived when we were nearer Land's End, and, in perfect weather, our little convoy arrived safely at Falmouth.

First, there was an ugly argument with the pilot on the subject of where to put our charges. The Harrison ship drew about forty-five feet forrard, and did not want to anchor; but the matter was soon settled, and we left them there in order to get on with our work-up.

One of the advantages of the new ship was that she had just been fitted with a new radar set working in the centimetric band, which had good discrimination and was able to detect submarines on the surface with ease, and even periscopes in good weather. Better still, the Germans did not realize that we had sets working on this frequency and they had no search receivers to give them warning of our approach. Aircraft of Coastal Command were also being fitted with centimetric-wave sets and the Germans were to suffer some heavy losses when surprised by aircraft when on the surface. The new set was easily trainable and also comparatively simple to maintain — a most important quality.

I felt much happier. It had been clear for a long time that the U-boats were attacking ships, both in convoy and sailing independently, not from periscope depth as we had expected, but on the surface. Owing to their small, low silhouette, they were very difficult to see at night, and heavy shipping losses had resulted.

In 1918 Doenitz himself had tried this tactic, and in 1939 he had published a book in which he urged the merits of the attack on the surface at night and hinted at the pack attack. So we should not have been caught so unprepared, but no one who mattered could have read either the history of the First World War or Doenitz's book. Consequently it came as an unpleasant surprise to find that U-boats were penetrating the convoy screens undetected and then lying stopped, still on the surface, in the middle of the convoy, picking off the unfortunate merchant ships one by one as they passed.

All peacetime exercises had been designed to counter submarines attacking from periscope depth. Any suggestion of attack on the surface, when echo detection was unlikely, had been dismissed with the hope that the asdic set would act as a hydrophone and hear the diesel motors of the attackers, but in practice this was not possible near convoys where the noise from many ships' propellers made detection of the U-boat by hydrophone almost impossible.

Improvised efforts to 'turn night into day' by illuminating the whole area of the convoy with starshell and fireworks were unsuccessful, and, in any case, always came too late to prevent initial attack. But with a centimetric radar, it would be possible to detect the U-boats as they came in on the surface to attack, and so stop the massacres.

Another advantage of the *Wolverine* was that she was fitted with a weapon called 'hedgehog' which had only just come into service. It threw a salvo of twenty-four small bombs about a hundred yards ahead of the ship (if my memory is correct) and provided a much more accurate method of attacking submarines than did the depth-charge. When attacking with depth-charges which were dropped from the stern or thrown out from the quarter, the asdic set often lost contact with the submarine several hundred yards before reaching the spot where the depth-charge pattern was to be fired. In the 'dead time' between losing contact and firing, the U-boat could and usually did carry out violent avoiding action which upset one's estimate of the boat's course and speed and so ensured an inaccurate attack. U-boats were very tough, and it was necessary to place a depth-charge within a few feet of the hull to make sure of a kill. Moreover, one needed to get the depth right too, which was not easy, as estimation of depth at that period of the war was a matter of guesswork mixed with experience.

In other words, the depth-charge attack, though stimulating to carry out, impressive to watch and terrifying to receive, was not nearly so dangerous or lethal as had been hoped and expected.

This had been appreciated in 1918 and plans made to design a weapon which would throw a depth-charge ahead of the ship and so avoid the dead-time errors. But in peace nothing was done and the idea was resurrected after the start of the war! The weapon came to sea in 1942 and, despite some initial adverse reaction from types who liked to dash in to attack at high speed and then hear a good bang, it proved successful. One attacked at slow speed and it was very much like a cat-and-mouse game. Also, as the fuses were contact-operated, one heard nothing if one missed until the whole salvo hit the bottom.

The rest of the work-up passed slowly. The exercises were rather an anti-climax after our first operational trip, but I don't think we wasted much time. The bad weather had been a valuable experience. Except for one or two who were hopeless cases, the sailors had found their sea legs, and we had been able to locate and get repaired many leaks. Reckoning we were now ready for the main job, we sailed to join our newly formed group — eager for the fray.

8. CONVOY TO MALTA

THE *Wolverine* belonged to a Special Group which, consisting only of destroyers — albeit of an ancient vintage — was used for fast troop and other special convoys. I was delighted at the change of job because I had become tired of the slow Atlantic runs which I had been carrying out in the *Sabre*. In summertime fast convoys were good value; it was in the winter they became such a menace. Then there was a continual struggle in one's mind whether to try to continue with the convoy, risking weather damage, or to reduce speed, and hope to catch them when conditions improved.

In mid-summer we were due to take part in a Russian convoy from Iceland to Murmansk and we actually sailed for Seidisfjord, where the ships were to assemble, but the disaster of Convoy PQ 17 delayed the sailing. We returned to Liverpool, somewhat relieved, in truth. It was only later that I realized how much I would have liked to have been able to say that I had taken part in a convoy to Russia!

We also did one or two trooping jobs, after which we returned to Liverpool to clean boilers and to grant some leave. The advantage of Liverpool over Londonderry as a base was that London was a comparatively short journey away; so I took advantage of the fact to go home for a few days. When we got back, there was a strong rumour of something on; Captain D had been giving our high-angle gunners some extra drills, and the whole ship became keyed up for the coming escort.

Our first job was a simple one: to take three large cargo-liners up to the Clyde, their assembly port. Air attack was the only possible danger, a fact which did not affect us seriously, as each ship had a far more powerful high-angle armament than we carried. We acted merely as a radio link for passing raid warnings to them.

On arrival next morning, early in August 1942, we were given an anchor berth which proved, to my horror, to be in the middle of a large crowd of destroyers of all types ranging from the mighty ships from the fleet to our old escort type. I had not picked up an anchor berth properly for ages. Usually we dropped the hook in a likely-looking spot and fixed our position afterwards. However, if we were to be back in the fleet, we would do things 'proper naval fashion', so we took great pains to approach slowly and to get into exact position.

Captain D signalled that the convoy conference would be held that afternoon — an interval which gave Number One a chance to remove the traces of the coal dust of our last berth, while I took the opportunity to call on one or two friends whose ships were lying near, in which we exchanged news over a glass or two. Then ashore for a dull routine conference, to be followed by a well-staged and interesting affair in the hangar of the cruiser flagship. The Commanding Officers of escorts and the Masters of merchantmen, with their liaison officers, were spread around two vast tables to listen to the Admiral's short talk on what was to come. He stressed the importance of Malta as a vital link in our Mediterranean chain, and followed with considerable details of the routes, formations and plans which would be carried out. Then the party split up into the various forces concerned, and points of still more detail were discussed.

We 'short-legged' destroyers had to sail early to top up in the Foyle before joining the convoy off the north of Ireland, so the five of us sailed as soon as possible, arriving in the Foyle about midnight, when we spent a jolly hour or so struggling for berths alongside some busy oilers in a crowded anchorage. By dint of great effort and much expenditure of language, all ships managed to sail on time without damage. There is a strong tide, it is a narrow river and some of the ships at anchor did not show the riding lights they should do. In bad weather the place was a nightmare.

Soon after dawn we joined the convoy, which was forming up slowly, taking up our position on the screen while from all directions cruisers, battleships and carriers converged on us. Before long the whole force was formed up and the first leg of the long journey had begun.

There were no incidents of any description, the weather being good and the enemy not appearing to have heard about the expedition. After some days the destroyers started to fuel from the big ships, an operation which I had only carried out before from a slow tanker by the astern method. From a cruiser at much higher speed and fuelling alongside, it was more difficult, while, to make matters worse, we were oiling from the Flagship, on whose bridge could be seen glimpses of the Admiral. It was the last straw when we saw Commander Anthony Kimmins grinning at us: 'If we make a mess of this, we'll be on the B.B.C.' But all went well and we rejoined the screen without disaster.

Some days out some more carriers joined, making the biggest concentration that I had ever seen. They spent one day carrying out exercises together, the Swordfish and Albecores representing the enemy, while the fighters practised interception and the ships exercised their anti-aircraft organization. The spectacle was inspiring, and must have cheered the convoy, though one attack by a squadron of Swordfish coming out of the sun caught us completely unprepared, and was a sharp lesson both to radar operators and to look-outs.

The weather was very hot, with a scorching sun over a blue sea. Most of my ship's company had never been as far south as this before, so strict orders were issued about avoiding sunburn. It was unfortunate for discipline that the Captain caught the sun worst of all.

Then we went to Gibraltar and we were fuelling there while the convoy passed the Straits under cover of a darkness accompanied by a thick fog. Owing to the fog, our party did not enter harbour in that close order which should be the custom, but they all got in after a reasonable interval!

It was a tremendous feat of organization to get all the ships fuelled, at the same time leaving the convoy adequately protected. Malta having little fuel left, the operation had been planned to take place without any ships topping up there, and a floating 'pumping station' was established in the middle of the Mediterranean for anyone getting short. In addition, secrecy was almost impossible because the Germans and Italians kept a large party of official spies established in Algeciras, across Gibraltar Bay, and these could watch all comings and goings. The problems of planning were therefore difficult.

The night after sailing for Gibraltar, I had a narrow escape from ramming a lateen-rigged felucca which was hiding its white light behind the sail. It was mistaken for a U-boat by the Officer of the Watch, who, quite rightly, increased speed to ram. We passed it very close, and must have given the crew the shock of their lives, while the lessons learnt on the bridge proved invaluable later on. By next day our force was about thirty miles astern of the main convoy, when masts were sighted ahead. As we closed, we could identify them as two destroyers with a tug in company. What were they doing? Were they hunting a U-boat? The next thing was a signal from the *Laforey*: 'Am picking up survivors of *Eagle*, close me,' and soon it could be seen that boats were down and that all three ships were crowded with survivors. The tug was an astounding sight. She had so many men on board that some were even up the rigging. She was literally hidden by a mass of bodies.

The *Malcolm* was detailed to help with survivors, while the other four of us carried out an unsuccessful hunt for the U-boat which had torpedoed the *Eagle*. After an hour-or-so's search, we set off for the convoy at high speed, soon to pass the tug, the gallant *Growler*, steaming alone flat out to rejoin a convoy whose speed was only a little less than her own maximum. That particular part of the Mediterranean was within easy flying range of Sardinia, and there must have been other U-boats about — but the *Growler* appeared undaunted.

Soon the convoy was sighted ahead over the horizon. There seemed to be great activity. Fighters were patrolling overhead, carriers were zig-zagging at high speed, and there was a continual coming and going of destroyers between the screen and the fleet tankers.

We took station astern, preparatory to our next job, which was to screen the *Furious* while she flew off Spitfire reinforcements to Malta, and then to escort her back to Gib. As our party arrived, one of the cruisers on the starboard beam opened fire on a shadower on the horizon, quickly followed by other ships, while fighters dashed out to intercept. It was an impressive sight which had brought the whole ship's company on deck to watch, but we could not wait to see the result because there was other work to be done and the survivors from the *Eagle* were to be transferred from the *Laforey* and her companion to some of the *Furious*'s screen for quick return to Gibraltar — an operation which was quickly carried out in a flat calm sea by the ships concerned going alongside each other.

All the 'Spits' got away all right, landing safely at Malta, except for one which had to make a forced landing on another carrier. It was the pilot's first deck landing, the machine was not fitted with the necessary gear, yet he succeeded in getting down with only minor damage.

Our little party then took up station on the *Furious*, which turned to the westward, leaving astern this determined force on whom so much depended. Of their subsequent adventures, losses and eventual partial success I have only read; suffice it to say that they saved Malta from almost certain surrender, and the tanker *Ohio* gained great glory.

The weather was still perfect, enabling us to make good speed towards home. The *Wolverine* was on the starboard side of the screen, being stationed between the Senior Officer, *Keppel*, who was ahead of the carrier, and the *Malcolm*.

That particular night was dark with no moon. Some time in the middle watch the alarm bell in my sea cabin rang, sending me leaping up to the bridge. 'Radar contact bearing green two O,' said the Officer of the Watch. 'I am altering towards as it can't be the *Malcolm*; we are on the starboard leg of the zig; depth-charges are ready.' The radar contact could only be a U-boat, or perhaps another fishing boat. I ordered 'Full ahead together' and steadied on a course to intercept. We were doing fully twenty-two knots before the increase so the range closed, very rapidly. At about a thousand yards the Officer of the Watch, whose eyes were well accustomed to the darkness, sighted a shape, then a bow wave; and I was able to throw off to starboard in order to ram. When three cables away I could identify 'it' as a U-boat about to cross our bows, and ordered the small bridge searchlight to be trained on her. Events moved like lightning. A small adjustment of course. 'Report to *Keppel* to the wireless office and 'Stand by to ram' to the depth-charge party. These were all the orders there was time to pass. The signalman on watch reminded me to ring the alarm gongs for 'Crash stations'. Then the U-boat was only fifty yards ahead. 'Switch on ten-inch' and 'A five-hundred tonner, I think' and WUMP...! At twenty-six knots we hit her fair and square at the after end of the conning tower. Long hours of practice had reaped their reward and our dreams had come true.

The shock was terrific. The ship seemed to come up all standing, the impact throwing off their feet all those not holding on tightly, we seemed to lift out of the water, then silence, followed by a heavy explosion. 'No depth-charges fired,' reported the quarterdeck, so that the noise must have been the submarine blowing up. 'Not much doubt about that one,' I said, and a lake of black oil began quickly to spread over the sea in confirmation.

She must have been caught unawares, because she was in full surface trim when we hit. And this was all for the best, because a diving submarine is dangerous to ram; as she may damage the bottom and propellers as the ship slides over her.

Then I had a moment to survey the situation. The first thing sighted was the *Malcolm* astern, who had seen the sparks flying when we hit and was investigating, and the *Furious* steaming past on the port side. The W/T[2] office just had time to get off an amplifying report before all power failed. At the same time Chief came rushing on to the bridge to report that the engine room had had to be evacuated owing to a burst steam pipe, but

---

[2] It might be as well to explain here that W/T means morse radio communication and R/T means voice radio communication.

that the boilers were undamaged. He had shut off steam and was waiting till the engine room cleared.

The Stoker P.O.s in the boiler rooms showed great coolness in a most terrifying situation. At high speed these huge spaces, filled with the roar of rushing air and separated from the sea by only a thin sheet of steel, were awe-inspiring to the most unimaginative mind. The first sign of trouble was the ringing of the alarm gongs, which warned them to stand by for a crash of some kind. After the bump, which was particularly shattering below the waterline, the men were unable to get in touch with the empty engine room; but steam was calmly shut off, and a stoker sent up on deck to report that the boilers were undamaged. Then the P.O. Telegraphist reported 'Ready to transmit with batteries', so I sent off another report to the *Keppel* asking for a ship to escort and probably tow us.

The *Malcolm* was sent back to our help, but by the time she returned, Chief had reported that he would shortly be able to steam on one engine, so I asked her to screen us as it seemed better to have one ship screening rather than both hampered by a tow. The *Malcolm* agreed, and circled us for the half-hour before we got under way. Soon after the bump, Number One came on to the bridge to find us all extremely pleased with ourselves. I have never forgotten his first remark, which instead of 'Oh, well done, sir', proved to be 'Oh, Lord, what have we hit now?'

There was a shocking mess forrard. The bows had been pulled down until the 'bull ring' in the eyes of the ship was under water; the stem piece, despite its twenty-five-years life, was intact; the fore foot had been pushed up through the ship's bottom into number one central store; the foremost lower mess deck was flooded, but the bulk-head abaft it seemed intact, and the Chief Stoker was soon at work shoring up, using the shallow-water diving gear. There were no casualties, although a few days later the Chief found that he had broken a couple of ribs. He had been thrown across the wardroom when we hit and had come into violent collision with the corner of a refrigerator.

The engine room reported 'Ready to proceed', and, after a little experimenting with the wheel in order to counteract the effect of one dead propeller, we set off at a thankful six knots in the general direction of Gib. It was a long way to go and the situation was not too bright, but we were all so bucked with the ram that nothing seemed to matter. At the time I thought that our victim was a German and hoped that we had sunk the torpedoer of the *Eagle*, but later it seemed more likely that she had been an Italian and records show this to be true.

A little after dawn the *Malcolm* was detached to hunt a U-boat which an aircraft was attacking to the north of us, but our solitary state did not depress us. It was only when the exhilaration wore off that we realized how naked our position was, and to encourage us, a passing Sunderland reported that a large trail of oil stretched for fifty miles astern of the ship — a result of leaks from the forrard oil tank.

The anti-submarine instruments had been smashed beyond repair, but the remaining electrical gear was in full working order. During the forenoon we worked up slowly to about eight knots by Dutchman's log;[3] causing the dead propeller to trail around for the first time.

There was a good deal of peering over the foc'sle at the wreckage under water, which could be seen clearly through the blue sea, and someone noticed a strange affair hanging down

---

[3] To use a Dutchman's log, a piece of wood is thrown over the side and the time taken for it to pass over a known length of the ship's side is measured.

from the bottom. After lengthy consultation it was decided that it must be the cable, which had fallen out of the smashed cable locker and from which four shackles were trailing below us. The ship would anchor herself before getting up harbour. As the supply steampipe was broken, a hand capstan was rigged, and with the aid of a purchase to haul it through the worst parts, Number One succeeded in getting all but a few feet of cable on deck. Our troubles were over at dawn next day, when we were met by an escort of two corvettes. Number One spent the day getting the ship cleared up, retrieving kit from the flooded mess decks and preparing for a ceremonial entry into harbour — for I was determined to put up a good show, both in appearance and in the method of getting alongside.

The hands were fallen in on the upper deck; the stoker's mess, which was temporarily on the oerlikon gun deck amidships, was cleared up, and everything was now shipshape. A tug met us outside the harbour, but I spurned it, hoping to get alongside before it could catch us up again. The ship passed the boom and shaped up for the jetty, making a perfect approach. Only the outer screw was working, so the stern would swing in when the engine went astern. It should have been just right, but my nerve failed me at the last moment and I went astern too soon. The stern swung in, the bows swung out, and it looked as if the tug would be needed after all. Then that hand capstan proved its worth — a hawser ashore, a quick run round the capstan and, just as the tug arrived, we were safely alongside.

We then sat down to await a dock for repairs. Rumour followed rumour, and one 'galley buzz' decided that Gibraltar dockyard would do the full repair. This would mean no leave, and that was an unpopular move, so I was much relieved when it was decided that, owing to pressure of work, the dockyard would put on a temporary bow to last only until arrival in a U.K. port. Then came a time of maddening waiting. The number of dry docks was limited, and convoy 'Pedestal' had sent several ships back in urgent need of repairs. Both the *Indomitable* and the *Nigeria* had been hard hit — the former by bombs on the flight deck and the latter by a torpedo below the water line. The *Nigeria* entered harbour very early in the morning with a heavy list and was soon put in dock for repairs. The *Indomitable* arrived during one forenoon in perfect weather with the hands fallen in, band playing, and presenting the most inspiring spectacle. Only close inspection showed the damage, which was heavy, but she had kept on flying her aircraft until the end. We were very proud of the navy!

The *Wolverine* seemed always to be the last on the list, despite my constant visits to the Chief Constructor's office with ingenious suggestions as to how he could fit us into a dock. Otherwise time passed very pleasantly. After three years' service in northern latitudes, it was wonderful to lie in the sun in between dips in the sea at Sandy Bay. Number One took up the sport of fish spearing, with more damage to his toe, however, than to the fish concerned. We played a lot of hockey, producing a useful team out of a ship's company in which only a half-dozen had ever played before; and other games flourished.

Our final effort was when we staged a pentathlon with the cruiser *Charybdis*, a grand ship with whom we had a great *entente* and who provided water-polo pitches and games gear, even allowing their band to play on board. The result of this tourney, which consisted of over a dozen events, was adjudged to be an honourable draw, although it was in the sports like darts and uckers (the naval ludo) that we gained our victories, rather than in football and water polo.

We also took the opportunity to see a good deal of the Coastal Command squadrons based on Gib. The R.A.F. were often on board — visits which resulted in one or two parties of no mean magnitude.

All my officers, including the doctor, went for flights — an experience which was of excellent value. Unfortunately none of us met any excitement in the way of U-boat sightings, but luckily we also avoided the 'neutral' French from Morocco, who seemed to take delight in attacking passing planes. But I had great fun one day as a passenger in the air escort of part of the fleet returning to the British Isles. My group Leader was one of the destroyer escorts, so I grabbed an Aldis lamp and sent him some messages about the station-keeping of the screen. Later I took even more pleasure in telling the fleet Flagship that her signalling light was badly trained.

The torpedo gunner had the most shaking experience. He went out in a Catalina flying-boat on a sweep which should have taken about seven hours; but on the way they were diverted to hunt a submarine. So Guns, on return from his first flight, had already spent twenty-four hours in the air.

There was a surprisingly large number of non-swimmers on board who were given training astern of the ship. They had every incentive to pass their test as soon as possible, because the water inside the harbour had a liberal coating of fuel oil which made bathing a doubtful pleasure.

A majority of the ship's company were H.O.s (Hostilities Only) who were originally rather a weedy lot. It was a pleasure to see the way in which they filled out and came on generally under the influence of sun and plenty of exercise. What pleased me most, however, was the way in which these Hostilities Only men of ours settled down to what was, to all intents and purposes, a peacetime naval routine. The ship was immobilized, so we arranged training classes, paraded guards, organized daily P.T., and turned the ship abaft the damage into as near a yacht as possible. Number One started by painting ship, then scraped off some of the 'bright work', which had been covered since the war started. For a week the sailors could not quite understand what was happening — then suddenly they were seized with a terrific pride in the ship, and after that we had to stop them scraping off the paint or they would have burnished over all.

Once in dock, the yard made us a false bow in a remarkably short space of time, and soon there were only a couple of days left before we could start. Passengers were embarked, including one Sapper officer; mails placed on board, and at dusk one night we set off for home.

It was not a pleasant journey: we had no escort, for no ship could be spared, and owing to our poor fuel endurance the route ordered was much too close for comfort to the French coast where the German bombers were based. But we hoped that the enemy would not worry about such small fry, and that no U-boat on passage through the bay would by chance bump into us.

It was difficult to know exactly how much speed the bow would stand. The Chief Constructor had, rather naturally, been most guarded on the subject and had restricted himself to assuring us that this was the fifth bow he had put on ships which had all arrived safely.

The weather was excellent for the first night, allowing the ship to make good speed. The corner was turned and course altered to the northward, along the Spanish coast, and then the trouble started. We should have reduced speed earlier. But we were all keen to get home quickly, making it somewhat difficult to decide to ease down. A northerly wind got up, followed by a moderate chop, which sent Chief hurrying on the bridge to ask me to slow down.

Some plates had cracked as the ship pounded into the waves, with the result that she began to fill up fast forrard. The portable pump had been already rigged in case of such a contingency, and the unfortunate stokers had just time to clear their meagre kit from the mess deck before it was again flooded, for the second time in two months.

Now followed an extremely long and tiresome five or six days. The pump ran continuously throughout this period, except for a few bad moments when the filter choked. The filter was cleared eventually, and we had again learned the lesson why it is so important to keep the bilges of a warship spotlessly clean. We certainly blessed the makers of that pump, which must have exceeded greatly its designed endurance.

The weather remained unfavourable. Wherever we altered course the wind followed, remaining ahead or on the bow and so reducing our speed to about three or four knots. The going was often easier on one leg of the zig than on the other, so that we increased on that leg and reduced on the next — a procedure which nearly reduced the Sub, who was trying to keep a dead reckoning position, to tears. Luckily the same bad weather lowered visibility, and we never sighted a plane, nor, apparently, were we sighted by a submarine, throughout the passage.

Our soldier passenger did not appreciate the motion, but we gave him full marks for his determination. He had been given an action station on the bridge in charge of the stripped Lewis-gun and despite a ghastly pallor, he never missed the 'exercise action' which was carried out daily.

All things come to an end, and eventually we were able to alter course to the north-east for the Scillies, thus putting the swell on the beam and enabling speed to be increased. Then some luck came our way, because we arrived off the Scillies at the same time as the cruiser *Penelope*, who was on her way home from her repair yard in America. A formidable fighter patrol had been sent to escort her up Channel, so I asked her by signal if we could proceed in company, so sharing her protection.

After some rude remarks about our bow, *Penelope* approved, and we took station ahead. The wind had now backed to the westward and decreased, so that it was possible to make a good speed again with the bows higher in the water and no bumping forrard.

Off the Eddystone we parted company and proceeded to Plymouth. The sea lay a flat calm, I increased to twenty-four knots to show the soldier what we could do in good conditions, and by noon the *Wolverine* was secured alongside the Flag Staff Steps, with an anxious ship's company making numerous inquiries as to when leave was to start.

9. COMMAND OF A GROUP

WHILE waiting at Plymouth, in the autumn of 1942, for the repairs to the *Wolverine* to be finished, I was kept very busy. After my leave, the first thing was to take a course at the Western Approaches Tactical Unit at Derby House, Liverpool.

Much has been written about Captain Gilbert Roberts who ran the place and it should be enough here to say that he was the ideal man for the job. He did invaluable work by careful analysis of records, he detected new enemy methods of attack, he invented new search schemes for finding U-boats and he helped to weld groups together. But, above all, he made a number of very stupid officers really THINK, sometimes for the first time in their lives.

In the navy we so often get our priorities wrong, and I was no exception, I fear. For the first few years of the war, the Home and Mediterranean Fleets got all the best officers and it was considered somewhat unfashionable to be in the Western Approaches Command, which, as a result, received many of the failures from Scapa Flow, many retired officers and many incompetents. There were a few young lieutenants in their first commands and a very few more senior officers to support the reserves who were such splendid material, but the good regulars were desperately few. Admiral Sir Max Horton, who joined in November 1942, was able to make many changes and to introduce new faces at sea, but the Battle of the Atlantic had then lasted three years and many million tons of shipping had been lost — some unnecessarily.

Gilbert Roberts succeeded in improving everyone who came to do his course, and this was his greatest achievement. I went whenever I could find a week to spare and, later on, took the Captains of the ships of my group with me, for he combined a vivid imagination with a good tactical and technical knowledge and a theatrical flair for getting his points across.

One evening, in November 1942, I was sitting in the Athenaeum, a pub in Plymouth which was then a useful place to meet one's friends and exchange yarns about the war, when my First Lieutenant bustled in and said that I was to telephone the Admiralty Appointments people at once. It was after nine o'clock but I found the Commander concerned in his office and he was quick and precise.

'Go back to the ship, pack, catch the ten-thirty to Glasgow and report to Captain D Greenock at ten o'clock tomorrow morning,' he said, 'and, oh! yes, buy a brass hat on the way if you can.' This was evidently no ordinary pierhead jump and unless the part about the brass hat was a joke, it seemed that I had a good job coming. We poured ourselves into a taxi and got back on board in a few minutes. There was not time for fond farewells and I just caught the train in a flurry of emotion and alcohol. The *Wolverine* had had a grand ship's company with a splendid First Lieutenant and my days there had been very happy. In fact they were the last carefree days of the war, for some heavy responsibilities were ahead and the light-hearted delights of driving destroyers on my own were over for ever.

Next morning I learned from Captain D Greenock that I was to take over a very *ad hoc* group which had been formed specially for the North African invasion and that we were to take a big, slow convoy to Gibraltar and bring back another one, empty, to the U.K. The group was to consist of two of the new twin-screw frigates, the *Tay* and the *Wear*, two R.N. and two R.C.N. corvettes, four fleet minesweepers and four

Bangor-class minesweepers. It was a thoroughly mixed bag, the ships of which, with two exceptions only, were entirely new to convoy escort work, while only four of the Commanding Officers had ever done the job before. The Captain of the *Wear* was a Commander R.N.R., officially senior to me, so it was thought that I should embark in the *Tay*, whose Captain was a Lieutenant-Commander. I was, by the time I arrived in Greenock, an acting Commander and feeling very pleased with myself.

The convoy was due to sail in about six days and there was clearly a great deal to do first. I had to try to get a staff officer to help me with the paper work. I had to get the Captains together and explain my ideas to them, and even more important I must get the senior signalmen and wireless ratings together to make clear to them what they had to do. And, above all, we must get to sea and carry out some exercises as a group.

It was a busy and difficult period. Most of the ships were at anchor in the Clyde so that getting hold of people for meetings was a frustrating and irritating affair. Many ships had defects to put right and several had not expected to go to sea before the departure of the convoy, and did not approve of all the exercises! However, with the aid of the Captain D and his staff who were helpful, we were able to complete most of my plans, though the sea-going part showed how much improvement was needed before the group could do more than offer a physical obstruction to U-boats. Both the radar and A/S sets of most ships were unreliable and the standard of training low. Communications, too, were paralytic and it was a hair-raising affair exercising fourteen ships in the Firth of Clyde in variable visibility at a very busy period of the war. However, I was as pleased as punch with my job and well rested after my leave;

the Captains were mostly very keen and we avoided disaster and improved greatly before finally sailing.

Communications were the key to success and R/T communications in particular. In those days the sets were not good, nor was the drill, and the maintenance men were inexperienced. It was quite an occasion when we made a signal and received thirteen immediate replies in the right order and I do not think that it ever happened during the first week.

The most cheering aspect of the situation for me was the fact that the *Tay* had a high-frequency direction-finding radio set (H/F D/F). I had never been shipmates with one of these remarkable instruments before, although I had heard much about them. By some means which I never was able to understand, we were able to get bearings of radio signals made in the high-frequency band by the U-boats, who did not seem to hoist in the fact that we were listening to them. The set was quick and accurate and was able to give a rough indication whether the transmitting submarine was near or far, though, of course, unless there were two ships so fitted and 'cross-cut bearing' could be obtained, the 'fix' was in no way accurate.

This might be the time to explain shortly the ideas behind the German Wolf Pack attack, which proved so successful and which Doenitz had developed with such tenacity, both in peace and war.

Control of all U-boats was exercised from a central headquarters by high-frequency W/T signals which could be received all over the Atlantic by U-boats on the surface or at periscope depth with an aerial sticking up out of the water. Moreover, as Captain Kretchmer writes in one good German book on the U-boat war, signals could be sent to U-boats which were completely submerged on what he calls 'ultra-long-wave radio'. So, unless the boats were very deep, contact with the shore headquarters could be maintained at all times and an efficient control ensured.

Each U-boat at sea reported its position daily to the shore and when the position of a convoy was established, either by an aircraft sighting, by a U-boat report or by the breaking of an Allied cypher, one U-boat would be ordered by Doenitz to act as contact keeper. This boat shadowed the convoy on the surface, making frequent reports by high-frequency radio of its position, course and speed, while the headquarters ordered all other U-boats within reach to close the shadowed convoy. Occasionally, the contact-keeper would home his colleagues, using medium-frequency radio which is easier to direction-find, but this was dangerous as it gave the show away very quickly. When enough U-boats had reported that they were in contact, and not before, the order was given from shore to attack. They went in at night and on the surface and sometimes there were so many around that they ran into each other! Each boat reported the result of its attack as soon as possible to the shore, together with the number of torpedoes remaining, and would then be given further orders. Day attack submerged would usually follow and the battles went on for days until contact was lost or until Doenitz called off the pack.

The U-boats could only keep up with the convoys by steaming on the surface using their diesel motors, because the batteries could not drive these boats fast for more than a few hours before running down. Thus aircraft were of tremendous value to sweep in the vicinity of shadowed convoys and, by forcing the U-boats to dive, so make them lose touch.

The high-frequency direction-finding (H/F D/F) set, in conjunction with aircraft, thus became an essential weapon in dealing with the pack attack, for if the contact-keeper could be heard and its bearing determined, it could be driven off or forced to dive and lose touch. There was then a chance that the rest of the pack would miss the convoy. It was not easy, however, as the U-boats had a choice of wave-lengths to use and we had to be listening to the right one to get an initial detection of an enemy report.

We often wondered why the Germans talked so freely, and after the war I had an interesting talk with an officer who had attacked one of my convoys and who is now a senior Captain in the German Navy. I asked him why they had talked so much, for although communication was the essence of the pack attack, they could have easily cut down the length and number of the radio reports, and so made their detection more difficult. He replied that they did not realize that we were able to direction-find their signals and that they had been told that the probable cause of the detections we were making was 'radiations by their radar search receivers' which were supposed to alert us to the presence of the U-boat. This was complete nonsense and showed that the German scientists had a remarkably poor appreciation of the facts.

Fortunately for the ships of the convoy, which was numbered KMS 4, the passage to Gibraltar was something of an anti-climax. The weather was reasonable and the enemy did not appear, although we had some anxiety over domestic matters in the convoy, such as smoke, lights at night, straggling, and so on. But on the whole it was a very peaceful passage, which was just as well, as many of the group had their asdics out of action on arrival. Only three or four ships had high-definition radar, which was the only type of any use for detecting surfaced submarines, and, moreover, the four Bangor-class minesweepers were too small for the Atlantic and could not possibly be described as efficient convoy escorts.

They did their best and it must have been very hard work, but the results were of little value.

I had been most relieved that during our passage through the Bay of Biscay we had not been sighted by a Focke-Wulf aircraft. For a short period in 1940 when the Air Group concerned had been placed under the control of U-boat headquarters, good results had been obtained by the Germans by co-operation between aircraft and U-boats. The aircraft would sight the convoy and report its position, often circling it and sending out homing signals on medium-frequency radio to help the U-boats assemble. But we now know that early in 1940, Goering, who resented any of his aircraft being under naval control, persuaded Hitler to reverse the decision, and co-operation, fortunately for us, thereafter declined.

Much skill is required both in navigation and communications to get good results from aerial reconnaissance, and all those concerned must work together and exercise frequently over the sea. This did not happen, and the full potential of the aircraft in helping U-boats to find their convoys was never developed. Doenitz tells harrowing tales of the aircraft navigation being so bad that when they sighted a convoy they were ordered to transmit on medium-frequency radio. All U-boats in the vicinity then took bearings on the signals which they dispatched immediately to the shore headquarters, together with their own position. Thus the convoy's position could be fixed, but at a great cost in breaking radio silence.

Fortunately, too, Coastal Command worked very closely with the navy and, while never, naturally, liking being under naval operational control, appreciated that it was necessary.

After a few sunny days at Gibraltar we met Convoy MKS 3 from Algiers, in the Straits — this time with less escorts, for some of the group had gone on to join the North African campaign.

I transferred in a whaler to the Commodore's ship while we were off Europa Point. This was a good but hazardous move, for while the Commodore was pleased to see me and we had a useful talk about policy, the whaler's crew was dreadful and I would never repeat such a frightening performance.

This time the enemy were to leave us alone again, but the weather more than made up for Doenitz's lack of interest. Two days after sailing, a first-class gale appeared and remained with us for nearly a week. The convoy got badly split up, the Bangor minesweepers became unmanageable and had to heave to, and I did not see many of the ships again though they all arrived safely. The *Wear* took in tow a ship which had lost her propeller, and altogether a most disagreeable passage was had by all.

On arrival at Greenock the group disbanded and I went off on leave, a good deal wiser as a result of my experience. For one thing I had at last realized how lucky I was to be in the Western Approaches Command and how important the Battle of the Atlantic was, and I promptly stopped intriguing to 'get back to the fleet'.

A few weeks later, in December 1942, I got command of my own escort group. It was the finest job in the navy for a new Commander — my acting brass hat was made permanent on 31st December — and I was naturally delighted at the prospect. I had had much convoy experience and was full of confidence; what is more, the group was to be based at Londonderry where I had many friends and which I knew well. Indeed, it suited me admirably as I wanted to get better acquainted with a Wren member of the Tactical Unit staff, but romance has no place in this narrative.

B 7 Group had been badly cut up in a recent convoy action, the Leader and his ship had been sunk, and the group virtually disbanded. Despite the set-backs, the ships, three of which I had worked with before, were in great heart. There was the *Tay*, there were four corvettes each with Reserve officers in command, and one destroyer, the elderly *Vidette*, recently converted to 'long legs' by the substitution of an extra fuel tank for one of her boilers. She was the only fast ship then in the group, could make about twenty-five knots on two boilers and her Captain was a Lieutenant who was, besides myself, the only regular officer in command in the group. Two of the corvette Captains were Australians, there were Canadians and New Zealanders in the party too, so we had a good Commonwealth team.

My own ship, the destroyer *Duncan*, was refitting in Tilbury docks, so I and my small staff — consisting of an asdic specialist (a bosun), a navigator as operations officer, a H/F D/F specialist whom I also made communications officer, a radar specialist and a few communications ratings — were accommodated in the *Tay*. The ship was horrified at the thought, but the arrangement worked well on the whole, due mainly to the tolerance of all concerned and especially the Captain, who always tried to make life as smooth as possible. These frigates were more comfortable than destroyers although they were slow and could only make eighteen knots, so that while I longed for the thrill of driving my own ship, there were temporary compensations in the situation.

All my staff officers, except for the A/S Bosun, were R.N.V.R.s and, except for the radar man, who was hopelessly sea-sick and had to go ashore, they knew their job and made a good team. The Navigator, who is now a schoolmaster, was a tower of strength. He was imperturbable and capable and provided much sound sense when my imagination got the better of my judgement. He was also useful as an 'observer' of ships of the group, where he had many friends and heard many things which would otherwise have missed me. I suppose he might have been called a spy, but I made all my staff officers tell me about the ships of the group which they boarded — and their job was to get around as much as possible. One had to know a staff officer well to act on his judgement, but it was often the only way to detect trouble in time to put it right before it was too late.

To sack a bad Captain might mean the saving of hundreds of lives; to disrate a bad asdic operator might mean the difference between sinking and missing a U-boat. In war, one should not pay too much attention to men's pockets, vanity or even to their material welfare. Kindness to incompetents seldom provided a dividend, whereas severity invariably paid. As Rommel said, 'The best form of welfare is hard training,' and in war, men at sea care little for such luxuries as ENSA and discussion groups. They want to stay alive, and although they will grouse about training, you cannot give them too many exercises so long as these are soundly planned and interesting. But the sailor will never admit it.

Londonderry had fine facilities for training and it was an excellent base. In addition to the depth-charge trainer where complete ships' teams could drill together, there were asdic trainers, communication classes and every other sort of training; and in 1943 an establishment called the Night Escort Attack Teacher was established, where asdic and radar operators on the bridge, communication, and plotting table teams — the brains of the ship in other words — were given realistic drills under conditions of darkness.

I was lucky to have an excellent Leading Steward who was transferred from ship to ship with me. Although by trade a head-waiter who had served both at the Savoy and the Piccadilly, he was a good seaman and a fine character to whom I became much attached. The other stewards in the ship were often seasick, but whatever the weather he was always able to compete both with my meals and with those of the wardroom. He also provided a certain continuity in one's movement from ship to ship, which made life more comfortable. He had the typical manner of the head-waiter and he was known universally by the sailors as 'Mister' Harvey.

For three months the group ran hard but had nothing to show for it but rust, and the only enemy we met was the weather, which was unusually bad even for the North Atlantic in winter. Although it was one of the bad periods and convoys were being attacked ahead and astern of us, we seemed always to steer clear of the wolf packs, which were then at the height of their success.

The Captains, with one exception who was too old and who had to go, were able and keen and we took our training exercises very seriously. Except for *Vidette*[4] they were all experienced in the Atlantic — *Vidette* had recently been First Lieutenant of a Mediterranean destroyer but he was quick to pick up the ways of the Western Approaches. We gradually became a good team, which knew what had to be done and how to do it, and all our training was devoted to two aims: to exercise the crews of the weapons, the detecting instruments and the communications; and to ensure that each Captain could deal with any situation which arose without having to be ordered to do so by signal.

---

[4] In naval terminology the Captain of a ship can be known by the name of the ship he commands.

After three months both the instruments and the weapons were working well. It had been a struggle, but much hard work had been done and we had been helped by the staff ashore. At last the Western Approaches Command was beginning to benefit from Admiral Sir Percy Noble's drive to improve training facilities and consequently the efficiency of the ships. Standards had been disgracefully low and there was much room for improvement. Moreover, Admiral Sir Max Horton, who had a quick way with incompetents — of whom there were plenty — had just taken over command. Things were improving.

In particular, it was hard to keep the asdic operators alert during these long uneventful passages. The noise of the 'ping' of an asdic set is a natural soporific and my sympathies were with the men who had to keep awake. I found that only by continual 'briefing' by the Officer on the Bridge was it possible to keep the operators interested and up to the mark, and in practice we had, quite unofficially, two states of readiness. The normal state, when we did not think that any U-boats were around, and the special state, when we had warning of U-boats and when it was necessary to strain every nerve to hear an echo.

On one run to North America we took out a B.B.C. commentator, Stanley Maxted, who hoped to describe a convoy battle, but unfortunately the only action he saw was an unequal contest with a large iceberg at which, for the interest of the gun crews, all ships had a smack as they passed. On another trip Wing Commander Henderson, who had a wide experience of Coastal Command work, came with us to look at the problem from the surface side. But he too proved a Jonah, and we saw nothing but a succession of gales. But he left us well satisfied with his journey and flew back to Scotland in less hours than he had taken days to come out.

This is a fine opportunity to remark on small ships' bases, for I worked from no less than nineteen during the war and my views on their conduct provide a hobby-horse which I ride whenever possible.

One soon reached the stage at which, before securing alongside or anchoring there for the first time, one could place a base into one of two categories. The first, and I am afraid there were quite a number of these, was the type run for the benefit of the sailors and Wrens ashore, where the ships took second place. Everything one asked for was a 'trouble', the ships were always in the wrong whatever we did, and we received the impression that we were unwelcome intruders on an otherwise happy and peaceful scene. The Officers in Charge were in many cases conscientious men who did their best as they saw it. They organized dances, they had excellent libraries, the schoolmasters flourished and current-affairs lectures were a regular routine; but all this was at the expense of the only job that really mattered, which was to make the ships 'ready in all respects for sea'.

Once, I entered harbour one evening after a long and important convoy battle, expected to be greeted at least with a request for an early report on our activities; instead we saw that the Naval Officer in Charge was attending a reception in a nearby ship, and seemed to be entirely disinterested in us. Next morning I reported to his office with my account of the battle, to be kept waiting while the Waste Disposal Officer, and the Red Cross representatives and the Chief Officer Wrens were interviewed in turn. With this Naval Officer in Charge first things did not come first. He was relieved a few weeks afterwards and the atmosphere in the base changed overnight.

The second category, and they were in the majority, were the bases where the Officer in Charge understood his job. One was boarded on arrival by a team of experts who asked what they could do to help. The shore staff worked night and day to repair defects. The training facilities were always ready when we wanted them. When we got into trouble, and this often happened, especially over accounts, the people ashore tried to get us out of it instead of finding some way of 'clearing their own yardarm', and when ships returned after a battle, the Naval Officer in Charge was always waiting to welcome them, whatever the hour of day or night at which they arrived.

Conditions at our Western Atlantic bases, Argentia and St. John's, Newfoundland, were not pleasant in winter. The temperature during our stay was seldom above freezing, sometimes reaching zero; snow blizzards were not uncommon and the ice in the harbour made manoeuvring ships difficult. During the outward passage, which was usually against the prevailing gales, many ships suffered weather damage of varying degrees of seriousness; while there was a great deal of rust to be removed and lubricating to be done. This upper-deck maintenance was not an easy job in the bitter cold, and in addition, it was important to give the ships' companies a rest after the buffeting they got in their small ships. However, the United States Navy, helped by a small British technical staff at Argentia and the Royal Canadian Navy in St. John's, gave us magnificent service, and the group would always sail in good trim after only a few days in harbour.

Once, it was necessary to keep men at the guns throughout the night for only constant movement would prevent them icing up, and the group sailed successfully in the morning. But within half an hour the guard rails, rigging and superstructure were covered with ice from the flying spume and moist air.

The sea was calm and ships well topped up with fuel, so there was no question of the stability being in danger. This was not so at the end of one west-bound passage, when, light in the water as we approached Newfoundland, we met a north-westerly gale, accompanied by very cold weather. Ice quickly formed everywhere, and the ship's movement prevented its removal as work on deck, especially aloft, was very dangerous. We began to get anxious. As the rolling increased there was much examination of stability diagrams, and it became necessary to flood some empty oil tanks with sea water — an unsatisfactory affair which meant much hard labour in harbour before tanks could be filled with fuel again. In those days we were not well equipped for cold weather.

Now, at the end of March 1943, it was a critical time in the Atlantic war, and losses had been very heavy with few U-boats sunk to show for them. In the official history, Captain Roskill writes:

> No one can look back on that month [March] without feeling something approaching horror at the losses we suffered. In the first ten days, in all waters, we lost forty-one ships; in the second ten days, fifty-six. More than half a million tons of shipping sunk in those twenty days; and what made the losses even more serious than the bare figures indicate was that nearly two-thirds of the ships sunk during the month were sunk in convoy... Where would the Admiralty turn if the convoy system lost its effectiveness? They did not know; but they must have felt, though no one admitted it, that defeat stared them in the face.

To add to our difficulties we were in one of those unpleasant periods of the war when the enemy were able quickly to decypher our codes and cyphers. They could thus get a good idea of the position of most convoys in the Atlantic and made good use of this knowledge. In his book, Admiral Doenitz says that he was also able to read the U-boat situation reports, so that he knew where we thought that his U-boats were! Fortunately for our morale, we were blissfully unaware of all this at the time. Roskill says that the Allies did not achieve unbreakable codes until June 1943, by which time much damage had been done. He also hints that our own code-breakers were not idle, but, again, we had no inkling of what went on at the time.

There was, however, one cheerful aspect to be recorded. At long last, support groups had been formed which could be used to reinforce the escort of convoys which were threatened or attacked. This idea had been considered earlier but shortage of ships had made it impossible to implement. Thus, when the escort-building programme was beginning to show results, the North African invasion demanded a number of special groups to take the invasion convoys to and from the Mediterranean.

Now, by taking one ship from each of the close escort groups, so reducing them to a total size of six ships, it was possible to form four support groups from the sixteen ships so released. At this time, too, the convoys to Russia had been temporarily suspended, and the Home Fleet was able to lend two groups of destroyers which were used in the supporting role. The decision to reduce the strength of the close escort groups required much courage, but it was correct, for we hoped that the support groups could be operated so that one of them was always 'around' when a convoy got into trouble, and the reduction in escort strength in fact took place only when attack was unlikely.

So, when we sailed for our convoy at the end of March 1943, we did not know it but the time of test was fast approaching.

10. THE BLOODING

ON 29th March 1943, the group, less the corvette *Pink* which had sailed earlier with the St. John's section of the convoy, left St. John's to join HX 231, a fast convoy of nine knots speed bound from North America to the United Kingdom. It was cold on sailing and the few exercises we had arranged were very hard work. By the time the group had passed into warmer air and water, the weather had got worse and there was a quick decrease in visibility. The convoy had reported that it would be late at the rendezvous, so the group was spread out at 'radar' distance apart at right-angles to the approach course of the convoy in order to give the best chance of finding it. We had one frigate, one destroyer and four corvettes.

A year or so earlier, in the days before radar had made life so much easier at sea, I received a sharp lesson in how not to 'meet'. The rendezvous for an east-bound convoy from Canada was a few hundred miles to the south of Iceland, from where I sailed in the *Sabre* in a moderate south-westerly gale. We did not see the sun or the stars during the run to the southward, and depended on dead reckoning for our position, so I aimed for a point thirty miles ahead of where the convoy should be met.

We reached the spot in filthy visibility and as I turned to the westward, thinking we were sure to bump into them ahead, I noticed a piece of white paper in the water close by the ship. Have they passed us? Are they ahead of station? Shall I turn to the east?

But I had not got the strength of my convictions and continued to the westward. After some hours it became clear that we had missed the convoy, which we did not catch up for some time. When I compared tracks afterwards I found that we had turned only three miles astern of them. My calculations of distance had been perfect, but the helmsman had 'bored to windward', so placing the ship to the westward of my estimated position; while to make it even more difficult, the convoy had been twenty miles ahead of schedule.

So now I set course for a point well ahead of the convoy, to allow for a large error in its estimated position, for the weather made it obvious that the ships would have been unable to get any sextant sights. As bad luck would have it, the convoy had been highly optimistic about its speed, with the result that after much anxiety we did not meet it until after dark. Aircraft would have been invaluable in helping the 'meet', but the weather in Newfoundland made flying impossible. It was a bad start to the passage.

We succeeded in taking over from the local escort, a Canadian group, after much signalling with shaded lights, and at dawn the *Tay* closed the Commodore's ship, the fine-looking Blue Funnel liner *Tyndareus*, in order to exchange papers and discuss the situation. The Commodore, Admiral Sir Charles Ramsey, who had been my Commander-in-Chief at Rosyth earlier in the war, was not pleased with his ships. They were certainly in a shocking state of confusion, and the group spent the rest of the day coaxing them back into position. The *Vidette* was sent astern to encourage the stragglers to greater efforts, the four corvettes closed in the scattered wings, and the *Tay* careered up and down the columns being polite to some ships and rude to others, with the primary object of counting them — not an easy job in that visibility.

I learned afterwards that the convoy had met rough and cold weather, and that station-keeping had become very ragged. The signal half-yards of all ships had frozen, the signal mast of the Commodore's ship had collapsed under the weight of ice, and the confusion was, therefore, understandable.

The convoy front which we had to protect from submerged attack was, as I have already described, over eight sea miles. The submerged speed of the U-boats was low, so that they had to attack from ahead or from the bow. The range at which we expected to be able to detect a U-boat on our asdics, even in good water conditions, was well under two thousand yards; when conditions were bad, which was normal in the summer months, the range was much less. It was thus impossible with the numbers of escorts at our disposal to form a 'fence' of asdic beams to protect the convoy. We had to rely on luck and bluff. The way to do it was to take the offensive at every opportunity, even the doubtful ones; the unexpected always paid, and the worst thing to do was to wait passively for an attack to start.

But the speed of HX 231 was high for trade convoys and gave the U-boats little time to get into position. There was no rescue ship and I had only one ship fitted with high-frequency direction-finding in my group. This meant that we could not get cross bearings of U-boats transmitting near us and so could not fix their position with any accuracy. With only one destroyer, one frigate and four corvettes, we were a very weak escort for a big convoy, but we had trained hard and were confident that we could acquit ourselves well.

By dark on 30th May all sixty-one ships had been rounded up and were in reasonable station. The group was then able to settle down to its main task — protection from the enemy.

All went quietly for the next three days, making us wonder whether anything would turn up to break the monotony of the last few months. On 3rd April the *Vidette* topped up with fuel from the escort oiler, a lengthy operation which is comparatively simple in good weather, but requires good ship handling and seamanship if the weather is bad. It was as well that she did, for she was to do much high speed steaming in the next few days and it is the speed which uses up oil so quickly.

Soon after the *Vidette* had fuelled, we heard a German control station answering a sighting report from some U-boat, but we did not hear the boat which was transmitting. A couple of hours afterwards, the Admiralty told us that a convoy, possibly one to the southward of us, had been sighted. I had one ship as an extended screen well ahead of the convoy by day, and neither this ship nor the *Vidette* whom I sent to sweep astern saw anything. We thought perhaps that it was the other convoy which had been sighted, but during the night a stream of signals was received from both bows, and it was only too clear that we had been sighted and that Admiral Doenitz had called in his pack. Air escort would have been of enormous value in preventing both the sighting and assembly of the pack, but this was before the days of escort carriers and of Mac ships. What is more, we were in the Atlantic Gap, which could not then be reached by aircraft from either Newfoundland, Iceland or Ireland.

I got a severe attack of that 'sinking feeling' which precedes most battles, and relief that the test for which we had trained so long was ahead was mixed with trepidation as to the result. There was then a rather disagreeable wait of nearly twenty-four hours while the pack assembled, and there was no attack that night nor during the forenoon of 4th April; but on that afternoon a smart crow's-nest look-out in the *Vidette* sighted a conning tower on the port quarter of the convoy. She went after the U-boat flat out, forcing it to dive and then she carried out a good attack, but the escort was such a small one that I could spare no one to help her, and she had soon to rejoin in order to be back in her station before dark. It seemed unlikely that the submarine had been sunk, but whether sunk or not we had put her head down for the time being.

The small number of escorts made any effective form of offensive impossible. All we could do was to zig-zag unpredictably and so try to deceive the enemy. The U-boats had grown considerably tougher and seemed to be able to stand accurate depth-charging. A successful hunt, unless one was very lucky, demanded a considerable period of time and at least two ships, and it was only when the support groups became effective that it was possible to detach ships to hunt to destruction. We were very cheered, therefore, when Sir Max Horton sent us a signal which said that one of the newly formed support groups had been detailed to join us. The 4th Escort Group consisted of four destroyers: the *Inglefield* (the Senior Officer) with the *Fury*, the *Eclipse* and the *Icarus*, the last being fitted with H/F D/F which would be a tremendous advantage.

There were two points which made me ponder, however. Firstly, the Group Commander was senior to me and I disliked the idea of giving orders to a senior officer — for the policy was, correctly, that the commander of the convoy escort, who had details of the situation at his finger-tips, should take tactical command irrespective of seniority. Secondly, the ships came from the Home Fleet, where, naturally, surface and air attacks were inclined to take first priority. As a result they were likely to be less well trained and certainly less experienced in purely anti-submarine work than the Western Approaches ships. But this is a digression, for the support group was still a long way away.

Before dusk the *Tay* and the *Alisma* had each sighted a U-boat, one on each bow of the convoy. The pack was drawing in and it was necessary to make plans for the night.

Many factors had to be considered, such as the direction and size of the moon, the direction and force of the wind and sea, the likelihood of there being any Northern Lights and, most important of all, the competence of individual ships and their Captains. The U-boats liked to attack on the surface at night, normally diving when detected; they were faster than the corvettes and their conning towers gave a small radar target and were extremely difficult to sight visually. So the problem of defence was not easy, as it was impossible to form an 'iron ring' around such convoys. Fortunately the enemy preferred to attack down sea instead of butting into it, and certain combinations of sea, moon and light allowed one to estimate the most likely direction of approach. I would then strengthen the dangerous side, and normally put my own ship in the probable hottest spot.

Once the decision had been made and the escort put into station, there was nothing I could do but stand on the bridge and wait for the inevitable attack, praying that the disposition for the night had been right. It was not an easy task and one on which so much depended. However, the group's radar and asdics were all working properly which simplified the problem — luckily, for heavy weather often caused damage to these delicate instruments. The wind and sea were from the north-west — on the port bow of the convoy, which was steering a little east of north. Accordingly, I concentrated most of the escort on the port side.

About an hour after dark a light was sighted on the port side of the convoy. The *Tay* investigated and found it to be a flare which had been dropped by a ship in the port-wing column.

There had been rumours of neutrals helping the enemy by showing lights and dropping markers, but this must have been a mistake and possibly a serious one for it took time to put out the light, which could be seen for miles.

About an hour later we sighted a flash on the starboard side of the convoy. It was a dark night, the Northern Lights had not yet appeared, and from the bridge the flash was taken at first to be a funnel on fire. There was an unforgivable delay in reporting the situation, and after seven very anxious minutes I asked all ships to report by radio telephone what was going on. Two minutes later the *Alisma* reported that a ship had been torpedoed, and another minute later the Commodore signalled that the leading ship in the twelfth column had been hit. Because of the delay, the counter action, which was to illuminate the whole area inside and around the convoy with starshell and flares in order to find the U-boat responsible, was too late. No trace of it was found, and I still do not know how it penetrated the screen. It did not come in on the port side however, and my dispositions had been wrong.

The distance between the *Tay* and the explosion was about seven miles so it was understandable that we had not been sure of its nature, but other escorts had been much nearer.

The unfortunate ship which had been hit was loaded with iron-ore and sank within two minutes. In the course of the search for the U-boat, we passed survivors who were scattered in the icy water, each with his red light burning. Some were on rafts, some were alone, but no boats had survived and it is my most painful memory of the war that we had to shout encouragement, knowing well that it was unlikely that they would ever be picked up. It was an appalling decision to make as to whether to stop or not, but by leaving her place in the search to do so, the ship would leave a gap through which more attacks could be made, and more men drowned. We had to go on. After the search plan had been completed I sent back the *Pink* to look for survivors, but she failed to find them and after four hours search I had to recall her to her station.

The search for the U-boat was also hampered by three foreigners in the starboard wing column who decided to break out of the convoy, thereby wasting the precious time of the *Tay* who chased them without success. The American was lucky to rejoin us next day, but no trace was ever found of the Swede and only one boat was picked up from the Dutchman. The pack picked them off at their leisure, and we learned again that the vicinity of a shadowed convoy is a death trap for stragglers. I suppose it was very frightening inside the convoy, where ships did not know what was going on and where every depth-charge explosion must have sounded like a torpedo hit. Ships must have felt very naked, too, when the illuminations were in full blast, for the object was to 'turn night into day'. But the Masters must bear a heavy responsibility, as they had been warned time and time again that the convoy was the safest place and that to break out was to commit suicide.

Before the escort had regained station after completing the search plan, there was another flash and a large frozen-meat ship, the *Waroonga*, reported by R/T that she had been hit aft but was maintaining station. She was the fourth ship in the fourth column and I think that the attack came from ahead and that the U-boat dodged between two escorts and passed between the columns, picking out her target at her ease. The screen by then was being rearranged to counter attacks from all directions and it seemed that the U-boats were attacking across sea and across the Northern Lights, which had just appeared. Soon we had another alarm, when the *Vidette* reported a contact astern of the convoy. This turned out to be only the tanker *Sun Oil*, who had one engine defective. She was miles astern but no escort could be spared to look after her and she too was sunk next day with no survivors.

About then a previously arranged alteration of course was carried out with which I had hoped to dodge the worst of the attacks. The situation looked grim, two ships torpedoed, one straggler and three others who had broken out, and there was still six more hours of darkness. I felt angry and disappointed, for we had not had a smell of the submarines responsible and it had been the delay in reporting the attacks which was to blame. I could not stop thinking of the men in the water astern and only after the report of the next attack had come in was I able to achieve proper concentration again. But all the next four attacks were driven off with the help of radar and a sharp lookout, and although there was no time in each case to do more than a quick counter attack and then rejoin the screen, the U-boats achieved no more success that night.

The group had settled down now, communications were good, there were no delays, and we were shaking the submarines, if not sinking them.

At dawn the *Tay* closed the *Waroonga* to discuss the situation over the loud hailer. She was keeping perfect station and all hands were extremely cheerful. Indeed, from the port side the only sign of trouble was a knot of men on deck huddled in the lee of a deck house, each with his little pack of belongings. On the starboard quarter, however, there was a hole through which a car could have been driven. The Master wished to transfer all men not required for steaming the ship, to an escort, but the sea was becoming rough making boat work difficult and lengthy, and there was much doubt whether she would be able to catch up the convoy again. Such delay would have invited certain attack so the Master agreed to remain in the convoy hoping that the engine-room bulkhead would hold and that the weather would not get worse.

Then we carried out a check muster of the ships, so confirming our calculations of the night that only fifty-six were left. During the forenoon, I sent the *Vidette* astern to pick up survivors from the *Sun Oil* who had radioed a distress signal. The *Vidette* had strict orders that she must, whatever happened, be back before dark, and I am afraid she failed to find a trace of the ship.

By noon the *Pink* had rejoined, one of the culprits from last night was back in station and we received a welcome signal that aircraft from Iceland would be with us that afternoon. The weather had become perfect with a calm sea and good visibility, and the U-boats were chattering like magpies all around the horizon, our H/F D/F operator reporting one bearing after another.

I chose that moment to lose my voice, but this proved less of a handicap than I expected. Without it the atmosphere seemed to become calmer, and it was remarkable how much one could achieve by gestures or by the written word!

The Liberators from Iceland left their base at regular hourly intervals, but the first had its radio set incorrectly tuned and failed to receive our signals, which told it on what bearing it was approaching. The second was homed without trouble and, in fact, arrived at the convoy before his fellow. The first intimation of its presence was two columns of water appearing over the port horizon, quickly followed by the radio report, 'Am attacking enemy submarine, request assistance'. Letting my enthusiasm outweigh my wisdom, the *Tay* which was the fastest ship left with the convoy moved out at full speed. It was a painful lesson in convoy tactics, for five minutes after we had left the screen, there was an explosion and we saw an enormous column of water rising from a ship in the centre of the convoy. Turning back, we could see that the escort tanker, the *British Ardour* which had served us so well, had been hit forward. At the same time the Commodore signalled that another torpedo had passed ten feet ahead of his bows. A search for the U-boat was again unsuccessful I fear, for we could not spare much time, because we knew there were other U-boats ahead. Leaving the *Snowflake* to pick up the crew, the remainder of the group rejoined the convoy.

The *British Ardour* was an old ship which had been carrying kerosene for many years and her bulkheads were badly corroded. Although she was very lightly loaded she quickly caught fire, filled up and sank, and it was lucky that no one was lost and only two injured.

I am afraid that the attack had been made through the gap left by the *Tay* when we went after the Liberator's U-boat. I should have realized that with so much activity around the convoy no ship could be spared, but my excuse, such as it is, is that we were strongly imbued with the idea of hitting the enemy whenever possible.

The other aircraft then arrived — late, but very welcome, spending the short time that he could stay with us in attacking two submarines, on to which we had directed him, one on the starboard bow, and one on the beam. The first arrival also continued to do great work, finding more targets ahead and on the port bow. He reported that one of these attacks was a good one, and we learned subsequently that he had sunk U-632. But owing to fuel shortage, the last Liberator had to go all too soon, leaving us with the knowledge that we were well surrounded and certainly in for a tough night. To add to the gloom, the support group signalled that they would be unable to join until the next day, owing to heavy weather ahead of the convoy.

We laid on an early supper so as to be well fortified for the coming battle, and I changed into dry clothes and shaved, taking advantage of the first quiet spell we had had for forty-eight hours.

The remaining hours before dusk passed without incident, and the *Vidette* which had failed to find the *Sun Oil* and the *Snowflake*, with the *British Ardour*'s survivors on board, duly rejoined. A moderate wind had got up from the starboard bow so that it was easier to 'place the field' for the night. As a diversion, I arranged an alteration of course just after dark in the hope of making contact earlier than expected on one bow and of delaying the attack from the other side. We also carried out some long conversations on the R/T with an entirely imaginary third Liberator in the hope that the U-boats might be listening, and when it came to issuing orders for the night, I talked on the air to ten escorts instead of five actually present and arranged for all ten signals to be answered correctly. I shall never know if the ruse had any effect.

Once darkness had fallen, there was not long to wait for the first alarm, which, incidentally, came from the side to which the convoy had altered, and the *Loosestrife* on the port bow reported that she had detected a submarine coming in to attack. All did not go as well as it should have done, but she illuminated the boat, forcing her down and no torpedoes were fired.

The Captain was not up to his job and the ship was, as a result, much below the group's standard. He left shortly afterwards, and the *Loosestrife* soon caught up with the rest in efficiency.

A little later the first of eleven other attacks, all from the starboard side, arrived, and from then on there was never a dull moment to starboard. They came in one after the other, luckily never synchronizing their attacks properly, and they were met by the *Alisma*, the *Pink* or the *Tay*, who just had time to illuminate and attack, dropping a pattern of depth-charges before regaining station ready for the next attack. The log of the R/T conversations is great fun to re-read, and I clearly had trouble sometimes in prising ships off a likely target and making them rejoin the screen.

There were many incidents — the *Alisma* was narrowly missed by a torpedo, and the *Tay* and a submarine were equally surprised by a sudden meeting when a U-boat slipped out of the darkness across her bows, moving fast in the direction of the convoy. The radar had failed to spot it and it certainly had not seen us. It was so close that it was inside the *Tay*'s turning circle and the bridge oerlikon gun sprayed its conning tower as it passed and then crash dived. The *Tay* quickly picked up asdic contact, her depth-charges were well placed and there was a great red glow in the water, followed by a very heavy explosion. We lost contact at once and, assuming that it was a kill, we turned to regain station. It was just as well that the U-boat — it was U-635 we found out afterwards — did sink, because our steering gear broke down and we turned helplessly in circles for some minutes.

Another time, the *Tay* had a terrifying encounter with a ship which was behaving in a highly dangerous manner astern of the convoy. She turned out to be a *Prince* liner whose steering gear also had broken down; nothing could be done except to give her a course to steer on completion of her repairs, and fortunately she was in station by dawn.

On the port side there was only one attempted attack, to the disappointment of the *Snowflake* who had a dull night, but it was different on our side, where the *Alisma* especially was doing great work. As the night passed, the intervals between attacks grew gradually greater; and by dawn we were very proud to realize that every attack had been driven off.

Then came tragedy. The weather had got worse during the night and just before dawn the *Waroonga* reported that her bulkheads had given way and that she was abandoning ship. The *Loosestrife* was sent to her help, but the sea was so rough that one boat capsized with the loss of seventeen men, and the ship sank shortly afterwards. It was tragic that their gallant efforts to keep up with the convoy had been so ill rewarded.

At first light the *Tay* steamed ahead of the convoy, taking the place of the *Vidette* who had gone astern to screen the *Loosestrife*'s rescue work. Two minutes after reaching station our asdic operator reported 'Contact right ahead', and the ship prepared to attack. The operator deserved (and later received) full marks for his determination that the contact was a submarine. The 'ping' was not a very good one and I was rather sceptical and did not call the *Tay*'s Captain, who had just gone below for a quick wash. So the attack was not a good one and the U-boat got inside our turning circle; but we evidently caught his Captain bending because just as the order 'Stand by depth-charges' was given, the stern of the submarine emerged for a few seconds close to our bows. The officers on the *Tay*'s bridge were so surprised that they could not believe their eyes, and I was able to indulge in some picturesque language to convince them of what they had seen. The *Tay* tried to swing her stern towards the U-boat, but it was too late and the depth charges were not close enough. Moreover, owing to a slip in the communications drill, only five charges out of ten were dropped, so we did not think we had made a kill. The depth charge crews were tired after a long night at action stations, and the attack came just as they were changing from full to half crews.

During this incident the convoy had been steadily advancing upon us, with the result that the explosion of the charges took place between the Commodore's ship and the leader of the next column. Manoeuvring inside the convoy was tricky, but the *Tay*, who was livid at having missed the first attack, avoided the second ship of the column with difficulty, turned round and dropped one more pattern by eye — a full pattern this time.

It was the drill to drop a small smoke flare in the water to mark a depth-charge pattern. For some reason the ships of the convoy got it into their heads that this smoke belonged to the U-boat, for immediately a fusillade of shots and shell was sprayed from all directions. It was a most dangerous affair, and six-inch and four-inch shells and oerlikon and machine-gun bullets were ricocheting all over the ocean. Why no ship was damaged remains a mystery.

In the middle of this scene the day's first Liberator from Iceland arrived followed shortly by the support group, so that there then ensued an extremely busy half-hour of intensive signalling. It was necessary simultaneously to give the aircraft its orders, to answer the Commodore's signals, to organize a search for the *Tay*'s submarine, to give the support group a clear picture of the situation, and to report to the shore authorities. My voice was beginning to return, but the spell of activity retarded recovery! The low visibility did not help quick signalling, but after we had passed one long signal to the wrong ship under the impression that she was the *Inglefield*, all was done and the U-boat astern was turned over to the support group, who kept it down for an hour or so but failed to kill.

Events were now turning in our favour. I put one of the support group ahead as extended screen and kept the other three with the convoy as close escort, for two of them had their asdic sets out of action and they were not therefore much use to us; nevertheless we had two H/F D/F sets now and that meant much. The mist made it difficult for the submarines to keep in touch with the convoy, and several were caught unprepared on the surface by aircraft diving out of the low cloud. We spent an enjoyable day directing the aircraft on to their targets and, owing to their efficient help, the convoy was not attacked again. The H/F D/F set had proved itself to be worth its weight in gold. We knew roughly where the boats were from their contact reports and, at night, they always made a quick signal before going into attack — presumably to avoid collision with their friends. By day, however, when individual attacks only were made, they gave us no warning before coming in submerged.

That night, 6th/7th April, was quiet, though two ships of the support group homed on a submarine some miles astern and attacked it without success. There was only one alarm, when, sometime in the middle watch, tracer bullets were seen in the middle of the convoy and an escort hurried to investigate, for tracer is usually a sign of a submarine between the columns. In the mist two ships of adjacent columns had got very close to each other, and a keen gunner in one decided that a submarine was menacing him and let fly. The flap soon died down.

The following day, 7th April, aircraft were again with us in great force, and several more attacks on U-boats were made. Again the visibility was poor and no U-boat came near us. After another quiet night, with no enemy W/T traffic, we could relax; the U-boats had evidently lost touch and we were out of the danger area.

The enemy had been in contact with us for over four days and nights, and it had been an exhausting time. We were all very buoyed up by the results, however, and one soon forgot the bad patches. By the time we were off the north coast of Ireland the weather had cleared and we were able to indulge in some mutual congratulations with the Commodore and his ships. I had escorted many convoys up the North Channel, but there was a particular thrill in watching these fine ships, now formed in long lines, steam safely away to their unloading ports.

The final result had been three ships lost in convoy and three lost as stragglers, against two U-boats sunk and many more damaged. Considering the size of the escort, the lack of aircraft during the early stages of the battle, and the fact that a big pack had been assembled to attack us, the group had acquitted itself well in its first experience of pack attack.

In discussions with Germans after the war I discovered that the pack contained seventeen U-boats, of which seven claimed to have fired torpedoes; so that there was at least one miss, since only three ships and three stragglers were hit. In addition to the two U-boats sunk, U-294 had been badly damaged and forced to return to base, and I am prepared to bet that this was the submarine which so saucily showed its stern to the *Tay* on the morning of 6th April.

On arrival at Londonderry I went aboard the *Loosestrife* and the *Snowflake* to meet survivors from the torpedoed ships. They were most cheerful and appreciative; British, Lascars and Chinese, all had worked hard in the corvettes and had volunteered to clean, polish and keep watches. The last words of the Master of the *Waroonga* as he stepped down the gangway were, 'I had better be thinking of getting myself another ship.'

11. A LONG FIGHT

WE had just over a week in Londonderry after convoy HX 231, which had brought us our first taste of pack attack. There were many commitments and time passed all too quickly. I found my own ship, the *Duncan*, waiting for me, and there was much to do to take her over from the temporary Captain and to get to know her and her company. The officers and men were all new to me and most of them had never seen a convoy before, for the ship had been recommissioned after a long refit and had just worked up at Tobermory on the west coast of Scotland.

She was a Flotilla Leader of the 'D' class which had been built in Portsmouth dockyard in the early 1930s. She was well equipped with weapons and detecting instruments and also had the new 'hedgehog', together with a monstrously big depth-charge which was discharged from a torpedo tube. She had kept a couple of guns for use against U-boats and a couple of torpedoes in case a surface warship was encountered. She had all the latest asdic, radio, radar and H/F D/F sets.

But being designed for short sharp dashes out to sea with the fleet, her endurance was too short for convoy work, which was a source of endless worry.

The *Duncan* had spent a couple of weeks at Tobermory, where Admiral Sir Gilbert Stephenson had given her the thorough training which he had perfected during the years. Before sailing, it was necessary to see that everyone knew exactly what was expected of him and to ensure that the group ideas were clearly understood.

I had also to crawl about to see for myself her condition, a tiring and dirty proceeding which took all one day.

The reports and track charts of our last convoy battle had to be finished, and the problems which had arisen had to be worked out on the tactical table and discussed by all concerned, and I had to address a large audience of naval and air force officers on the last operation. It was particularly important to meet the aircrews who had flown so far to escort us, because although they had done great work, there was still a number of details to be put right. This is the only method which works. The correct official procedure of writing a report only stirred up a host of acrimonious minutes in headquarters and, in any case, never reached the men concerned in time to be of any value.

There were changes in the group. The *Loosestrife* had a new Captain and the *Sunflower*, also with a new Captain, had returned from refit, relieving the *Alisma* which was well overdue for a rest. So much time was taken up in talks with the newcomers in which we discussed every possible contingency. Another day was taken up by a flight to Derby House, Liverpool, to give Sir Max Horton a first-hand account of convoy HX 231 and to get the latest news of the Battle of the Atlantic. Time was pressing, and to cap it all I was in the throes of 'urgent personal affairs' which required careful organization.

Summer had not yet arrived. Weather damage was frequent and it was still a difficult task to produce a complete group at sea on the right day. Skilled labour was short, and all our technical devices were getting increasingly more complex. The last few days before meeting a convoy were often more tiring than the passage which followed!

During the winter, too, the *Philante* group training scheme had become fully developed, and very good it was. The yacht

Philante, now the Norwegian Royal Yacht, was stationed at Larne at the mouth of the Belfast Lough, which was centrally placed for escort groups from Londonderry, Liverpool and Greenock, for submarines from Rothesay in the Clyde, and for aircraft from the Northern Irish bases, both Royal Air Force and Fleet Air Arm. With the *Philante* representing a convoy, and the Rothesay training submarines acting as U-boats, complete escort groups and squadrons of aircraft were exercised together before convoy passages under realistic conditions, followed by careful analysis and discussion. Groups were welded together into teams, aircraft were able to carry out in practice the tactics on which they had been trained, and the results were excellent. It was a pity that it was not possible to start the scheme much earlier, for the Joint Air Anti-Submarine School at Maydown in Northern Ireland had also only just started work, and the combination provided excellent training.

This time we succeeded in getting out to the Londonderry exercise area with a complete group. We had one more ship than the last convoy — the *Duncan* — and we were confident that we would do better. We tried hard not to waste time during these exercise periods which were always too short and which were usually interfered with by the weather. The venerable submarines with which we exercised, last war models which had been condemned years before, were not always reliable and life was often frustrating.

In the main, however, everything went rather better than usual. The weather was good, the submarines kept going, and targets were in the right position at the right time, the aircraft were punctual and were equipped with radio sets which worked.

I had been horrified by the apparent difficulty of hitting a submarine at night at close range, for only the oerlikon gun had been any good against the U-boat which nearly scraped the paint off the *Tay*'s bows — so I designed an exercise to represent realistic conditions. The oerlikon gun was 20 mm. and was only effective against personnel. In exercise 'Pointblank' one ship towed at her best speed a splash target representing a U-boat's conning tower. The firing ship headed straight for her on opposite courses at full speed. At the last moment she steered so as to pass less than a hundred yards clear and on getting abeam fired at the splash target with every gun on board. We also tried throwing a live depth-charge at it, but the result was so dangerous that a special exercise charge had to be used instead.

For the towing ship, this exercise was alarming enough by day; by night it was suicidal. Usually some enthusiast would open fire too soon, and always at least one gun's crew, intoxicated with excitement and deafened by noise, would fail to see or hear the cease-fire signal and would continue to direct a stream of lead at the unfortunate towing ship. But we escaped damage and found the exercise of great value in teaching the guns' crews to shoot quick and straight.

Before sailing we had a final meeting in the anchorage at Moville at which the exercises were analyzed and the last points of policy discussed. A couple of trawlers were joining the group temporarily as rescue ships, and they, fitted with asdic, were a useful addition to the escort — which now would consist of two destroyers, one frigate, four corvettes and two trawlers.

There was the escort tanker to be visited, too. This ship, the *British Lady*, was fitted with buoyant rubber hose which she streamed astern and which we picked up and secured at our forecastle. Oil could be pumped through the hose at a reasonable rate, and once secured the operation did not take very long, perhaps two hours for a normal refuel. But picking up the gear was not easy, especially in bad weather, and station-keeping astern of the tanker was a difficult task. The *British Lady* and the *Duncan* had not fuelled at sea together, so on the way to meet the convoy we exercised the operation. It was as well that we did for many mistakes were made and much of the gear had to be adjusted. The *British Lady*, an old friend from the days of the Norwegian campaign, did us splendidly through the passage — though she had not been given enough fuel and we sucked her dry before the end. There was another escort oiler with the convoy, the *Argon*, but unfortunately she was fitted for oiling alongside and not astern and, worse still, she had canvas hose only instead of rubber. It was only possible to use her in a flat calm which we never experienced, and the one attempt to fuel from her nearly ended in disaster. Consequently we were not able to get at her precious cargo of oil, which was to have serious results.

By two o'clock in the afternoon of 22nd April 1943, we had found the convoy off Oversay, transferred documents to Commodore J. K. Brook, R.N.R., and discussed plans over the loud hailer. We had joined the various parts of the convoy together and we had settled down in our stations. The convoy was a slow one with a reputed speed of seven and a half knots (which it never reached) and consisted of thirty-nine ships. I spent the first four days, which were uneventful, steaming in the middle of the convoy in order to save fuel, for the *Duncan* had a bad reputation for oil consumption. Our chief concern was the weather, which held us up badly and threatened to make the passage a long one.

The ships, being light in the water, found great difficulty in station-keeping and the escorts were kept busy chasing them back into position. One night we could see no less than eight sets of 'two red lights vertical' from ships out of control due to the weather. On 26th April the inevitable happened and two ships collided with each other. One was sent off to Iceland unescorted and the other was able to remain in the convoy. It was not a pleasant prospect for a damaged ship to sail off alone, but no one could be spared to go off with her. I now know that she arrived safely.

That day the *Vidette* joined with three ships from Iceland. I was getting most alarmed about my fuel and asked our headquarters at Liverpool to arrange for me to nip into Greenland to top up if the weather continued to prevent me from fuelling at sea. Luckily on the 27th the weather improved and both the *Duncan* and the *Vidette* were able to top right up. It was a great relief for Greenland is in the ice pack at that time of year and it would have been a difficult journey. We also got some good air cover from Hudsons based on Iceland. About this time, 27th April, we heard that an east-bound convoy to the south of us was being attacked, the visibility dropped and our hopes ran high that we should miss the U-boats whom we thought would concentrate on a laden convoy homeward bound.

But at noon on 28th April we heard a submarine transmitting apparently quite close, dead ahead of the convoy. Visibility was only three miles, and I went out at full speed in the *Duncan* to see if we could find anything — we had no success. But it was certain by then that the U-boat must have sighted or heard us on her hydrophones, and it was clear that we were in for a heavy attack — again that horrible sinking feeling appeared.

I now know that U-650 sighted us in the morning and shadowed all day. In his report he complained that the zig-zagging of the escorts made shadowing difficult, but he also said that he got within two thousand yards of one destroyer ahead of the convoy 'which must have been asleep'! This must have been the *Vidette* and he was lucky, for it was most unusual for her to miss anything. Fourteen other U-boats were ordered to close the convoy and attack that night.

The weather was so bad that no flying from Iceland was possible and so we could do little to prevent the pack assembling at its leisure. A couple of hours before dark we sighted a submarine on the port bow. The *Duncan* was able to get quite close before it dived, but the high seas made an accurate attack difficult and I fear that little damage was caused. It was clear by then that the pack was going to leave the other convoy and concentrate on us. The night promised to be a busy one.

Placing the field was simpler than usual. The wind and sea were strong, making attack from abaft the port beam probable. Owing to the weather, an alteration of course was out of the question, for ships were finding station-keeping very difficult, so the *Tay* was left to deal with our U-boat, and we rejoined at high speed. I put the *Duncan* on the port quarter with other escorts ahead, on the port bow, on the port beam and astern, leaving the starboard side completely unprotected.

We were back in station before dark, the *Tay* shortly after that, and the stage was then set for the night's performance in weather which had just started to improve. There was little delay before the *Sunflower* raised the curtain with her report of detecting a U-boat coming in to attack from the port bow. She attacked it with gunfire, forced it down and then dropped depth-charges. By then it could no longer fire at the convoy, so the *Sunflower* returned to her station, for the enemy liked to lure away escorts leaving a gap for more attacks.

About eleven o'clock, a half-hour later, the *Duncan* detected a U-boat on radar and went straight for it, catching it unawares and getting in close before it dived. At the time, I had hoped that it might have been sunk by our pattern which had been very close, but there was no time to investigate. There were better things to do. As we turned to regain station, yet another U-boat was detected by radar also coming in down wind to attack. We turned towards it and this time the sea was directly ahead and although the wind had dropped the swell was still heavy. The speed increased, the ship moved into the waves, sending spray over the mast and drenching the guns' crews and everyone on the bridge. There was no question of surprising it, therefore, because it could see us coming for over a mile, and the U-boat dived quickly, making our depth-charge attack of doubtful accuracy.

The depth-charge crews on the quarter deck were having a very difficult time. The ship was pitching and rolling badly; the seas were washing down the quarter deck, soaking the men there, while the heavy and cumbersome depth-charges were difficult to reload. We were able to keep them aware of what was going on by a running commentary on the loud hailer. There is nothing worse than working on blindly, literally in the dark as to what is happening. The crews made no mistakes, however, and were quick reloading.

After this attack we found no sign of the U-boat so we turned again to rejoin the convoy, dropping another pattern in the area as we passed to discourage any idea of a premature surfacing. Once again, soon after starting back, there was a shout from the radar office 'Submarine green three zero', and again we were able to close down sea from astern to the submarine and get very near before it dived. It was a difficult moment. I could not decide whether we were going to hit or not. Ramming is a splendid method of sinking submarines, especially with the sharp bow of destroyers, but the rammer is left in a shaky state of health. The nearest harbour was nearly a thousand miles away and the convoy still had many days before it was safe from further attack. The escort could not afford the loss of its best ship, and I therefore preferred to refuse the chance — a decision which required more moral than physical courage to execute. Fortunately, however, the U-boat helped me to decide and got down quick, and I dropped an accurate pattern over the swirl of the conning tower. I had great hopes of that attack, although they were not shared by the Admiralty Assessment Committee.

For the third time we turned to rejoin. For the third time we dropped another discouraging charge *en passant*, and then to our amazement yet another U-boat was picked up on its way to the convoy. Like the second one it was up to windward, so that sheets of spray soon showed us up. It dived quickly and again our attack was a poor one.

After this last attack we succeeded in getting back to our correct station without interference and there was a temporary lull in the operation. There had been no opportunity to look at the ship's track during the attacks, but a quick glance now showed that there must have been four separate submarines involved. Apparently they had approached the convoy in line ahead in the hope that the leading boat would attract attention, leaving a free passage for the rest.

We were extremely pleased with the result. In less than an hour we had driven off four boats and we hoped that we had at least damaged two of them. It had been a very testing baptism of firing for the ship's company who had behaved splendidly, as I had the pleasure of telling them over the loud hailer.

The history shows that one of the U-boats which attacked us that night was badly damaged but got home and gave a good account of the proceedings. Another one, U-528, after being damaged in the battle, was sunk by an aircraft in the Bay of Biscay during its passage back to base. So we did not do too badly for a ship which had only just commissioned and was on its first operation.

Shortly after we had rejoined, the *Snowflake* piped up and reported a torpedo passing ahead of her. The submarine was sighted a moment later and at once attacked. Unfortunately there was, for the *Snowflake*, an unusual slip in the drill, and owing to a phonetic error the order 'Hard a'port' was not obeyed until too late. The U-boat got clean away, but the convoy was not attacked. While the *Snowflake* was thus engaged, we took her position on the screen, but there was only one more attempt that night, from astern, which was beaten off without difficulty by the *Tay*.

At dawn on 29th April, the *Tay* was sent back to sweep astern in case there were any damaged U-boats on the surface and to discourage shadowers. The convoy, still unscathed, was in good order and the weather was now better. After seeing that all escorts were in their day stations, I exchanged congratulatory signals with the Commodore and went below for a sleep. About five minutes after leaving the bridge, the alarm bell rang and I dashed back. 'Ship torpedoed astern,' the Officer of the Watch reported, and we could see that one ship had hauled out of the line to avoid her next ahead. The group at once carried out the routine search plan for the U-boat responsible. It was, as usual, extremely difficult to determine from which side the torpedo had been fired. One ship said one side, and another the opposite, while the victim signalled that she did not know. But the sight of the explosion in the water well outside the convoy was a great help, for another of the same salvo of torpedoes had exploded at the end of its run after passing through several columns without hitting another ship. I now think that the submarine must have fired from between the columns very close to her target.

After a short time the *Northern Gem*, one of the rescue trawlers, detected what must have been the U-boat responsible, but it was not possible to spare any ships for a prolonged hunt. After half an hour the torpedoed ship, an ancient American freighter which had maintained station without trouble, suddenly stopped and abandoned ship. The bulk-heads had cracked and the engine room had flooded. The *Northern Gem* was left to pick up the crew, the *Tay* was ordered to screen her, and the rest of us hurried back to station before the next attack. The *Northern Gem* rejoined some hours later with all the survivors except one who had been killed by the explosion. The Skipper was a North Sea fisherman who knew more about mine sweeping than convoy work, and when I asked him some pertinent questions I found that the charts which showed the route of the convoy had been left on board the wreck, which had not been sunk. So the *Tay* had to go back to make sure that the wreck had sunk or to collect the charts. As it happened, she found no trace of the ship, but she detected a submarine on the way back and spent some hours attacking it. The U-boat was tough and she did not succeed in making a kill, but the sweep astern had been well worth while.

There was no more excitement that day, 29th April, although we received the welcome news that the destroyer *Oribi* was joining us from Iceland and that another group of four Home Fleet destroyers had sailed to support us from Newfoundland. But they were a very long way off and it was clear from the radio traffic that at least three or four U-boats were still in touch.

I then considered topping up with fuel, but the weather had got worse again and it seemed too risky. This weather was astonishing even for the North Atlantic. It was uniformly bad throughout the passage, with short spells with no wind but with big swells, sandwiched in between the gales. Again the weather prevented any air cover being provided.

The night was reasonably quiet. One rather half-hearted attack was driven off by the escorts on the windward side, but prospects were gloomy because there was a long way to go to Newfoundland, the weather forecast was shocking, and the convoy seemed to get slower and slower.

There was another brief spell of calm next morning, 30th April, when the *Oribi*, which had joined during the night, was able to fuel. Unfortunately she was new to the game, the weather got worse during the operation, and she made such a mess of the oiler's gear that no one else could fuel that day. This was to bring serious consequences to my *Duncan*.

The *Tay* rejoined at dawn and the day was quiet. By the evening another full gale was blowing from ahead and speed was further reduced. Flying was dangerous, and the only aircraft which took off had soon to return to its base, so that we had no help to deal with the pack, who were holding on tight, waiting for better weather in which to attack. Nothing was seen of them that day, but during the night (30th April/1st May) an attempt to get through the screen was detected by H/F D/F and prevented by the combined efforts of the *Snowflake* and the *Sunflower*.

We tried to establish the rough position of the transmitting U-boat by cross bearings, we plotted it on the chart, and then when we later arrived near the position we dropped one or two depth-charges in order to discourage it if it was still close. The weather was much too rough to send ships out on a bearing as

174

we normally did, and detection by asdic in that sea was also impossible.

I remember one worrying incident during that night. We were dropping depth-charges in support of the two corvettes, an operation which was highly hazardous in that weather. We could only manage eight knots and it was necessary to set the depth-charges to explode deep, for at a low speed a shallow charge does much damage to one's own ship, because the explosion is too close to the stern. One of our charges went at about fifty feet, lifting the stern out of the water and causing leaks in the tiller flat. More serious still, the wardroom gin glasses were smashed — but the ship's rum and the wardroom wine had been carefully packed and avoided damage! The next morning I had to investigate the premature depth-charge firing. The man responsible was a respected and reliable elderly able-seaman of the best type, who helped to provide the backbone of a ship in those days of dilution. He denied setting it wrongly, and there seemed no point in arguing in those circumstances and we had no further trouble with our settings that commission.

The gale grew steadily worse all day, 1st May, until the wind was blowing like the bells of hell. The convoy was almost stationary and ships were heaving to as best they could, gradually spreading over the ocean as they drifted about mostly out of control. Two ships had to turn and run before the wind and we never saw them again, although I believe they reached Iceland safely.

The *Duncan* was hove to first with the wind on one bow and then on the other, and we could do little except make sure of keeping reasonably close to the Commodore's ship. It was most frustrating to see the convoy melting away before our eyes, but we could do nothing about it for at that time I did not understand how it was possible to heave to a convoy without much difficulty.

At noon on this day, 1st May, one of our old friends from 120 (Liberator) Squadron turned up from Iceland, a magnificent effort in shocking weather. But the U-boats were all sitting comfortably below the waves, waiting for the gale to stop, and he could do no more than confirm our worst fears about the convoy and give us the unwelcome news that there were icebergs thirty miles ahead of us. He added for good measure that if we continued on our present heading for fifty miles, we would be well inside the Greenland ice pack.

There was little to do except to pray that an improvement in the weather next day would allow us to alter course in time. In that twenty-four hours the convoy made about twenty miles progress; at times we seemed to be moving backwards.

To add to my worries, the Chief came on the bridge to report that the foremost tanks were leaking oil into the boiler room and that he had now to close down the forward boiler, which meant that we would have to rely on the after boiler room alone. I went down to have a look around and found the situation worse than I would have thought possible. A highly combustible mixture of air and fuel vapour filled the boiler room, several feet of oil and water were swishing from side to side of the bilges, and the unfortunate men on watch were sliding about on the slippery deck plates. It was a bitter thought that we had just come out of a long refit, and we commented most unfavourably on the managers and men of the firm which we had just left.

During the afternoon a Mitchell bomber, apparently from Greenland, passed several times over the convoy. He belonged to the U.S. Army Air Force and apparently knew no known language, nor could he understand signals flashed, made by voice or key, so he seemed of little use to us.

However, this aircraft had forgotten to switch off its navigation lights, which were merrily flashing and giving away its position for miles. I was worried, but the mistake had the unlikely outcome of making U-380 think that there was a new secret weapon in production, and he reported to Doenitz accordingly. So the aircraft was of more use to us than we thought!

It is now clear that Doenitz called off all the boats of group 'Star' that evening, as he did not reckon it was worth while continuing the battle; but of course one could not guess this at the time. I think that the weather, the aircraft and, I hope, the performance of the escorts all persuaded him that ONS 5 should be left alone.

After a worrying night there were signs of improvement in the weather in the small hours, and by dawn of 2nd May the sea was going down rapidly. The group at once set about collecting the convoy. Some of the ships were over thirty miles from the Commodore and the process was lengthy; but again a Liberator arrived from Iceland, flying over one thousand miles to reach us, and proving invaluable in rounding up ships. We blessed our forethought in sticking close to the Commodore's ship, for we were now able to form a nucleus on which the rest of the ships formed. The great question was whether we should be able to get them all together in time to dodge the ice pack which was in sight on the starboard hand. We just managed it, though many small growlers and isolated floes passed down the columns and the *Duncan*'s attempt to oil met with failure owing to the continual twisting and turning of the tanker as she avoided the ice.

By the time we were clear of the ice pack the wind had got up again and fuelling remained impossible. However, the situation, if still gloomy, was better, because we had collected most of the convoy — except for one or two odd ships and except for a group of five who were being chased along by the *Pink* some distance astern.

That afternoon the support group, consisting of four destroyers of the Home Fleet with Captain D 3rd Flotilla, in charge in the *Offa*, joined. Captain D had been at Liverpool when I had been in the *Wolverine* and I knew him well. It might have been embarrassing to give instructions to a vastly senior officer, but I made 'requests' and he complied with them in the most friendly way, and these unusual but necessary command arrangements worked quite admirably throughout the operation.

During the early part of the evening the support group split up into two parts and swept slowly out on each bow of the convoy. At midnight they were moved to a line-abreast formation, two miles apart and seven miles ahead of the convoy. At daylight two ships of the support group covered each side of the convoy at visibility distance, while the *Duncan* looked out ahead and the *Offa* swept astern — all with the object of forcing down any shadowers. But nothing was seen.

So there was a quiet night, except for the wind which continued to blow very hard indeed. The convoy crawled on into heavy seas and in the *Duncan* we were rapidly reaching the point when we had only enough fuel left to make Newfoundland at economical speed. I had to decide whether to leave the convoy or to continue and to hope for an improvement in the weather. On the one hand, the enemy was still in touch, and I did not want to leave my group at such a time. On the other hand, the weather forecast was very bad indeed and I did not like the idea of running out of fuel altogether and having to be towed, possibly at a very inconvenient phase of the operation.

After much heart-searching, I decided that the *Duncan* had to go. The weather would not allow boat work, nor transfer by a jackstay, so I had to go with her. Command was therefore handed over to Lieutenant-Commander R. E. Sherwood, R.N.R., in the *Tay* and we left at the best speed the weather would allow. After two days the wind shifted in our favour, we met an unexpected favourable current, and we managed to make St. John's with four per cent fuel remaining. We were most depressed because we felt we left the group in the lurch and were thoroughly ashamed of ourselves, though there was really no one to blame except the staff who had decided in the 1920s the endurance of such destroyers.

The story of what happened after we left on the morning of 4th May is probably the most stirring of convoy history. That afternoon three destroyers of the support group had to follow our example owing to fuel shortage, leaving the escort painfully weak. By cracking our cyphers Doenitz's radio intelligence service had established the position of convoy SC 128, which was east-bound in the general area of ONS 5. By some chance of fate all the U-boats which were directed on to SC 128 missed it, but ONS 5 was again sighted by the middle man of a big group, and soon no less than thirty boats found themselves unexpectedly in a most favourable position for attack. On 5th May the weather moderated somewhat and the enemy attacked with much success. That night and again next day, 6th May, more attacks followed with further successes, despite a tough defence, and altogether eleven ships were sunk without the loss of any U-boats.

There were no aircraft available which could reach the convoy, and by dusk the position seemed desperate, for there were only five of the close escort and two destroyers of the support group, the *Offa* and *Oribi*, remaining with the convoy. All ships were worn out after many days of bad weather and a running fight which had already lasted more than a week. There were over thirty U-boats in firm contact and the first support group, which had been sailing from Newfoundland to help, could not arrive till the next morning. All escorts were short of fuel and some of depth-charges as well. In the words of Captain D 3, 'The convoy seemed doomed to certain annihilation.'

Professor Samuel Eliot Morison, the official U.S. naval historian, says in his account of the battle that Doenitz realized that it was essential to attack in force that night, for the convoy would soon be under the protection of the air 'umbrella' from Newfoundland. So he exhorted his U-boats to make this final attack 'with the utmost effort', and he even ordered them to remain on the surface when attacked by aircraft and fight it out with the gun, in order to avoid losing touch with the convoy.

By the intervention of providence the convoy entered fog at dusk, and by a combination of skill, luck, initiative and sheer guts, the pack was heavily defeated. The enemy made twenty-four attacks that night, all were driven off, and not one more ship was sunk. The U-boat casualties were very heavy and four were sunk and three more heavily damaged during the course of the night. Two of these were surprised on the surface in the fog and were rammed, and two others were sunk by depth charges or 'hedgehog' attacks. In his report, *Tay* remarks, 'All ships showed dash and initiative. No ship required to be told what to do and signals were distinguished both by their brevity and their wit.'

All this time the *Pink* with her five ships was trundling steadily along astern. She had her troubles, but she got four of her charges into harbour and succeeded in sinking U-192.

Next morning, 6th May, the 1st Escort Group on its way to the convoy came upon some unsuspecting submarines and shook them severely, sinking one; and a Canso flying-boat of the Royal Canadian Air Force from Newfoundland also did some useful work and destroyed one.

At 9.15 a.m., 6th May, Doenitz called off both packs and ordered all boats to proceed to the eastward for replenishment. The convoy was still together and the longest and fiercest convoy action of the war had ended with a clear-cut victory. The passage from 'Oversay' to 'Westomp', where the local escort relieved us, took sixteen days, and the enemy had been in contact for ten of them.

In addition to the five submarines sunk by surface ships, two others collided, both U-boats being lost, so that for the thirteen merchant ships which the enemy had sunk, he had lost seven U-boats, with several others badly damaged, while the R.C.A.F. got another. German records recognize this battle as the turning point of the Atlantic war, and while I am very proud that ships of my group should take such a prominent part, I shall never cease to regret that I did not risk the weather and stay with them until the end.

This decision has haunted me ever since. It was entirely correct and based on common sense. I had been in the *Tay* with Sherwood during the last battle and I knew that he could compete. My own ship was new to me, just out of refit, leaking badly, and I did not trust the fuel consumption figures. The weather forecast was shocking.

It is now clear that Doenitz had no intention of continuing the attack — though I did not know it at the time — and this is some balm to my wounded vanity. Yet the weather did improve and I would probably have been able to fuel. As we have seen, Doenitz attacked 'by mistake' and I had missed the 'golden moment' which comes but once in a lifetime. And of course if I had had any idea that the U-boats were piling up ahead as they were, I would have stayed with the convoy and risked needing a tow to base.

Discussions after the war with the Germans were most interesting. They showed that no less than sixty U-boats were directed on to the convoy. Sixteen of Group Star sighted us on 28th April and four claimed to have fired torpedoes, though only one ship was sunk. As has been mentioned, two boats were damaged and had to return to harbour, U-386 and U-528, the latter of which was sunk by aircraft in the bay, so the attacks of the *Duncan* had at least done some good. On 3rd May, Group Specht, consisting of seventeen U-boats, sighted us, six claiming to have fired torpedoes during the subsequent three days. No less than three of this group were sunk and one was damaged. On the 4th a large group, Ansel, containing some of the Star Group, with twenty-four in all, made firm contact, but only one even claimed to have fired torpedoes and three were sunk. The last group to get into touch, the Drossel Group of sixteen boats, did not fare very well either. No boat claimed to have fired torpedoes, and two were sunk in a collision on 3rd May.

In his review of Admiral Doenitz's memoirs in the *Sunday Times*, Captain Roskill writes, 'The seven-day battle fought against thirty U-boats is marked only by latitude and longitude and has no name by which it will be remembered; but it was, in its own way, as decisive as Quiberon Bay or the Nile.' Professor Morison made the total fifty-one and I reckon that fifty-nine or sixty U-boats were engaged against us at one time or another, but this is a carping complaint to make about a generous and stirring tribute for which my group is both proud and grateful.

12. A CLEAN BILL OF HEALTH

WE were busy during our short turn-round in St. John's after the big battle. There was much to be celebrated and much to be discussed. There were many hours spent flogging out the track charts of the actions and the analysis of the eighty-odd attacks on U-boats, and the main report itself had to be written.

On 14th May 1943, as the first ship of the group slipped from the jetty to meet the next convoy, the last form was signed. I took it up to the local offices myself as I wanted to have a last look at the plot in the operations room where the situation in the Atlantic was shown.

There had been much to do in the ships. The *Sunflower* had rammed a U-boat and had had to be docked to get a patch put on her bow, very few ships had many depth-charges left — the *Snowflake* had arrived with one only — and all ships had minor defects to be put right after the appalling weather which we had met. In the *Duncan* we had been alarmed by the heavy rolling. The ship had many alterations during her refit and now she seemed to have too much top hamper. So we spent all available time searching for unnecessary top hamper which could be removed. When the ship left, the jetty was littered with steel lockers, electric cables, copper voice piping, and wooden fittings of every description, as well as the treasured accumulation which was prised out of the upper-deck 'cabooshes' (as the stores where the captains of tops keep their spare rigging and cleaning gear are called). The average petty officer hates throwing anything away, and the pile of rusty blocks, useless slips, and other gear, was a huge one.

To add to our troubles the ship in peacetime had been a flotilla Leader. With such a personage as Captain D on board, the leader found no opportunity to chip the layers of old paint off the ship. Captain D's ship had to be immaculate at all times. No ugly red lead could mar her beauty, so that endless layers of paint used to be slapped on with the resulting accumulation of unnecessary weight.

We set to at once, and the noises of the chipping hammers continued all day, while any defaulters were so employed during the evening. Knocking off paint is a slow process and we had not time to get rid of as much as we would have liked, but at least we felt a little happier about the stability on sailing.

A very elderly repair ship, the *Greenwich*, commanded by an even more elderly retired officer, was secured alongside in the harbour and proved of great help to all ships there. She was not so well fitted for her task, however, as the modern U.S.N. repair ship and floating dock in Argentia, and we used to say there that the bright lights were at St. John's, but Argentia was the place to get repaired. Later, however, a fine base was set up at St. John's.

After avoiding the icebergs which guarded the harbour entrance at this time of the year, we soon caught up the group which was already formed up, steering for the rendezvous. A few hours after leaving harbour we ran into the thick fog which one expected in spring near the Grand Banks, and the passage was an unpleasant one. Luckily we succeeded in meeting the convoy on time, for despite the fog, they were in exactly the right place. We met them at dawn on 15th May, the first confirmation of our radar's accuracy being the sound of their sirens booming across the water. It was not easy to take over from the local escort, which was led by H.M.C.S. *Niagara*, nor to exchange documents and information with the

Commodore, Captain J. Forsythe, R.N.R., but it was most important that the convoy should keep up to time, because I had a most pressing private engagement to keep at St. Mary's, Cadogan Square, two days after it was due to arrive, for I had somehow persuaded the Wren from the Tactical Unit to meet me there at eleven o'clock with the necessary witnesses, and it would not do to be adrift. I sent a note over to the Commodore to this effect, and received the reply that he had a golf match that same day and would do his best. He had a remarkable way with him, for the convoy got home twelve hours early, despite head winds for several days.

There were thirty-nine ships, not including the rescue ship *Zamalek*, all heavily laden, and the convoy was a slow one with a reputed speed of seven and a half knots. There was one escort oiler, the *Bente Maersk*. The convoy consisted of many old ships, most of whom were coal burners. The Commodore did his best to stop them making smoke, but he had little success. We used every kind of threat to back him up, but many of the firemen were new to their job, and as with station-keeping, smoke making does not seem to improve until the convoy has been attacked — when it is too late.

The fog persisted all day and we had considerable difficulty in keeping the ships together. We had been rather rude to one liberty ship which insisted on keeping about three miles astern of the rest, despite her ample speed. But when the Master replied, 'Listen here, Captain, not one of my officers has ever stood a watch before and I cannot stay up here all the time,' we felt very ashamed of our language. The tremendous shipbuilding programme in the States certainly produced some raw combinations of officers and crew, and many officers had gained their tickets by correspondence.

That night there was a particularly unpleasant affair during the middle watch. In the thick fog the *Vidette*'s radar picked up a large iceberg dead ahead of the convoy. There was no time to alter course, although in any case such an attempt would have been madness, for fog signalling by siren is uncertain and trouble would have been inevitable. The unlucky *Vidette* was therefore told to place herself between the iceberg and the advancing convoy, to stop engines and to make certain by all means possible that the ships should know all about the situation. She burned a searchlight, she switched on every light she had and she sounded the letter 'U' continually on her whistle to warn the convoy that it was 'Standing into danger'. I had some anxious moments as she escorted the berg through the columns, but all went well and we had no collisions.

During the night one of the ships, the *Tamaha*, deliberately broke out of the convoy and, owing to the fog, we were unable to prevent her from getting away. I never did find out why she left, as she did not have the courtesy to let us know, but I heard later that she had returned to Newfoundland.

Next morning, 16th May, the fog cleared for the first time since we had met the convoy, just in time to allow the *Sunflower*, who had undocked late, to make an accurate meet. We were now up to numbers, for a Canadian corvette, the *Kitchener*, which was on passage to the U.K., had replaced one of the trawlers which had been left behind. We had two destroyers, one frigate, five corvettes, and one rescue trawler, as well as a rescue ship — on the whole, a very reasonable escort for a convoy of some forty ships. The improvements in visibility allowed the Captains to get some sleep, for what with fog at sea and the report writing and celebrations of ONS 5 in harbour, we were all rather tired!

But after two successive and prolonged struggles with the wolf packs, the group was in the best possible trim. Each ship knew what the other would do in all circumstances and I had to make very few signals — ships acted at once and reported what they were doing. They never waited for orders.

The weather was perfect that day, and the destroyers and the *Sunflower* were able to top up with oil. There were no alarms, and only the rattle of the chipping hammers disturbed the peace aboard the *Duncan*. I had reserved 'B' gun shield for myself. It had a nice flat surface with no tricky bits and the paint flew off in satisfying sheets. The ship was chipping mad by then and every description of weapon had been pressed into service, ranging from pen knives to mauls. We must have knocked tons of paint off her. The visibility was maximum, the sky blue, and the sun was shining brightly. At one moment we were saying how good it was to have a warm day after eight cold months; the next, someone would remark that the convoy could be seen for miles and that we would be lucky to get through the patrol line without being sighted.

We had a Flying Fortress as air escort during the day whose value was rather reduced by poor communications. Relations between the air force and the navy in Newfoundland were not as good as they ought to have been, and we were reminded of the 'bad old days' of 1940 and 1941 in the Western Approaches Command. We did our best, with gin and good fellowship to put things right during our stays at St. John's.

The next morning, 17th May, an American tanker signalled that she had a man seriously ill on board, and after our doctor had diagnosed the case by means of a loud-hailer conversation, I asked the rescue ship *Zamalek* to take the man on board. She was better fitted than we were for dealing with such cases, and in a short time the operation was over and both ships were back in the convoy — to the disappointment of my Canadian doctor, who was always keen to use his knife.

It was a great thing to have a rescue ship with the convoy again, there never being enough of these invaluable vessels to go round. In addition to their chief job, which was the picking up of survivors, they helped with the sick, were very useful in passing signals, both visual and radio, and they were equipped with H/F D/F. In fact, with their wide experience of convoy work, they were almost as good as an extra escort although they had no means of offence. They were manned by the Merchant Service with a naval doctor and we got to know them all well, *Zamalek* being an old friend.

My ignominious retreat from ONS 5 still weighed heavily on my mind and I was determined to avoid any further incident of this type. The *Duncan* accordingly spent the first few days in the middle of the convoy, instead of zig-zagging on the screen, for the slow, steady course used up less oil than the faster zig-zag. Again we had air cover from no less than five Flying Fortresses during the day, but again their efforts were reduced in value by poor R/T communication.

On 18th May we had no air cover for some reason or other, and I took the opportunity of the perfect weather to fuel the *Kitchener, Snowflake, Pink* and *Loosestrife.* During the day one of the ships developed engine defects and I detached the trawler *Northern Spray* to bring her along astern and to rejoin if possible. The calm was too good to be true, and at eight o'clock in the evening we heard a U-boat transmitting on the port bow fairly close. I sent the *Vidette* out on the bearing. She saw nothing, but three hours later many more close-range signals were heard and it was clear not only that we had been sighted, but that at least four boats were already in firm contact. The last two battles had been preceded by some preliminary doubt whether we had been sighted or not, but this time there was no question of waiting for the answer.

It was rather like bathing in a cold sea from a slowly shelving beach when one runs and plunges into the water; previously it had seemed like gingerly wading in and prolonging the agony. I rather looked forward to a battle now, and there was no longer that sinking feeling of anticipation, for we were well on top of the enemy, we had a good escort and we were full of confidence.

The *Northern Spray* was quickly told to take her ship on to the stragglers' route, which was well clear of our track, for I did not want her to bump into any submarines shadowing us from astern.

Then I told the group all I knew about the position of the submarines, and we stood and waited.

It was not until about one o'clock in the morning of the 19th that we fixed a submarine transmitting only four miles away on the port bow, and I went flying after it in the *Duncan*. It was a bright moonlight night with a calm sea, and the U-boat must have seen us coming from some distance, as it dived at a range of 4,000 yards. We dropped a pattern of depth-charges on the spot by eye, as we did not get an asdic contact. In the meantime the convoy had executed an emergency turn to starboard, and I sat on the U-boat until it was no longer a menace, after which the convoy resumed course.

Just before dawn I turned the convoy ninety degrees to starboard in two turns of forty-five degrees, all ships turning together, in order to fox the U-boats waiting ahead for a dawn attack. The plan worked admirably, and we dodged several of them whom we later heard chattering away like magpies from a position on our original track, no doubt complaining bitterly at missing us.

As always, our friends the Liberators of No. 120 Squadron from Iceland were promptly on the job, and for a second time in a few weeks the first sign of the first aircraft was the splash of its depth-charges over the slowly lightening horizon. I had learned my lesson about detaching escorts from the convoy, and after telling the aircraft that no ship could be spared to help him, I gave him two bearings to investigate, each of which resulted in a sighting and an attack.

For the next twelve hours there was a never-ending series of attacks on submarines. First of all the *Tay* was sent off astern for one which the aircraft reckoned he had damaged. Within half an hour *Tay* was sending off 'Tally-ho' and had forced his boat to dive. *Tay's* attacks seemed to be good ones, but we learned after that he did not kill. A few minutes later, the *Snowflake* detected on her asdics a submarine coming in to attack from ahead of the starboard columns of the convoy. She counter-attacked at once and two officers on the bridge, to their delight, saw a periscope in the middle of the depth-charge pattern, but it was a tough boat and it did not sink. We joined the *Snowflake* and, much to her disappointment, took over the hunt, for a destroyer has more speed to rejoin and only one ship could possibly be spared. Our first pattern was dropped between the columns abreast of the second ships, which were badly shaken by the explosions. Our steering gear promptly broke down, but fortunately was put right quickly, for the ship had started to swerve towards one column and only 'full astern' could have saved us from a collision. Then the convoy passed on and we settled down to hunt.

The Captain of U-381 was a determined man and although he must have been damaged and was evidently unable to dive deep, he tried every dodge to get away. This was the first time I had had a chance to use in anger the 'hedgehog', which, as already described, was a weapon which fired twenty-four small bombs ahead of the ship; it was much more accurate than depth-charges but it had the disadvantage that, unless you hit, there was no explosion and you did not know by how much you had missed. I missed with the first shot owing to a bad estimation of the submarine's course, but the second attack scored one hit. It was most thrilling to stand, stop-watch in hand, waiting for the explosion — we saw oil rising and soon left the spot at full speed back to the convoy. On our way reports kept streaming in. The *Tay* was rejoining after her attack, the *Pink* had had a good crack at her boat and was returning, and *Sunflower*, correctly, had decided that the convoy was too lightly protected and had left his target to be dealt with by aircraft. A new Liberator had just arrived and the *Vidette* was setting off to help the first aircraft, which had run out of depth-charges.

The signal department was kept very busy. As we approached the convoy there were two large explosions in the water about two miles away. I still have no certain explanation, but the probability is that one of the submarine Captains did not like the idea of pressing in his attack and had decided to fire into the blue, hoping that his claims would not be too closely investigated. It was not a brave attack. We came up through the columns at high speed, the signal 'KILL' flying at both yardarms, and we got some cheery waves from the ships as we passed.

At about eight o'clock, just as we had regained station, the bridge telephone operator sighted a conning tower on the horizon ahead. It is astonishing how often a casual onlooker will sight things at sea before look-outs. I believe look-outs are born and not made and there was little doubt that ours had been somewhat unlucky in their heredity. We went flat out after this boat and the convoy did yet another turn to avoid the danger area. Once more the U-boat dived quickly, and having sat on it long enough to be satisfied that it was no longer a danger, we rejoined. A third aircraft had by then arrived to relieve the first, which was short of petrol. I knew the new Captain and was able to warn him to use depth-charges only on sitting targets as otherwise he would run out of ammunition. We quickly gave him three bearings to look at and within ten minutes he had no less than three submarines in sight. So, after a short and amicable discussion as to which he should go after first, during which he made the classic statement on R/T, 'As Mae West said, one at a time, gentlemen, please,' he succeeded in putting all their heads down without trouble.

After that the tempo eased down, thank goodness, the enemy W/T stopped altogether, and we had time to look at the plotting chart, to study the tactical situation and to think about the next move.

It had been a very busy scene indeed in the chart house where we kept a plot, for we were receiving a stream of bearings from the H/F D/F operator which had to be plotted and interpreted by the H/F D/F officer; many R/T signals were coming in from aircraft and escorts which needed reply, there were signals to the shore headquarters to draft and I had also to dash away from time to time to carry out an attack on a submarine myself. Fortunately the First Lieutenant, who was an asdic specialist, was well capable of looking after the bridge until the last minute, when I took over the ship and he the earphones, for his ear was much better than mine.

From a quick appreciation it was clear that there was still a large number of the enemy around us, about thirty we thought, but not one had succeeded in getting through yet, and there seemed no reason why they ever should, if we continued to have an air escort in daylight.

With three ships fitted with H/F D/F I was able to get fixes on U-boats transmitting near us with great accuracy and to send the aircraft quickly off after them. Moreover, the *Zamalek* operators were highly trained and well experienced radio officers and produced splendid results. My team was good, and very keen, but they were all young telegraphists on their first few months at sea and they could not have had the same experience as the rescue ship officers, who always produced the best results. About then we also received the welcome news that a support group of four frigates, the 1st Escort Group, was closing us at full speed from astern, and by the afternoon they were signalling that they had met some of the team from the morning brawl and were busy polishing them off. The *Wear* and the *Jed* had a torpedo fired between them, but they succeeded in sinking the culprit, and it must have been most depressing for the submarine Captains to surface for repairs well astern of the convoy after a frustrating morning's work to find yet another team of ships bearing down upon them from a quite unexpected direction.

That afternoon, 19th May, both the destroyers fuelled from our efficient Norwegian oiler, for the aircraft seemed to have got the U-boats' heads well down for the present and the night promised to be a busy one with plenty of high-speed steaming. I remember that fuelling well. The Prime Minister was making one of his great speeches, and we rigged a loud-speaker on the bridge in order to hear it. But the attempt was not very successful, for the effort of keeping station on the oiler and of directing the activities of both aircraft and escorts was too much for proper concentration on the speech. We were very pleased, however, that he was reserved but quietly confident about the U-boat war. At one of the tensest moments of the last convoy, I had gone below to eat a quick supper and, having switched on the American news, had heard that an eminent Admiral had claimed that the U-boats had been driven off the seas and that the Battle of the Atlantic was over. With the certain knowledge that there were well over twenty submarines hard on our tail and another six days of attack in prospect, I was inclined to mistrust the optimism of the great.

After we had topped up, the *Vidette* came to fuel and, shortly after, owing to an aircraft sighting a U-boat ahead of the convoy, another emergency turn by the convoy was necessary. I had been dreading this all afternoon, since altering course when fuelling is a tricky business. *Vidette* coped skilfully, undeterred by my rude signals — he and I had often argued whether it was a possible manoeuvre and there was now no doubt about the question. The long rubber hose was intact after the turn had been completed and his station keeping had been perfect.

The aircraft continued to keep the pack at a respectful distance, making many more attacks throughout the day. I was told to detach the *Kitchener* during the afternoon, and off she went to join a west-bound convoy. Before dark the support group caught up and after an exchange of news were given their positions for the night. Wind and sea were just right for the opposition, but it was easy to place the field, for the most probable direction of attack was clear.

There were four ships in the 1st Escort Group, the ex-U.S. coastguard cutter *Sennen*, and three frigates, the *Wear* which carried the Senior Officer, the *Jed* and the *Spey*. I kept the cutter on the close screen, for her silhouette was more like a liner's than a warship's and she could be seen for miles, while the others were placed well clear of the convoy, one up moon, one up wind and the other well ahead. Two of the ships were fitted with H/F D/F and we were now able to get most satisfactory results with the five sets present.

We all thought we were in for a bad night because conditions for the submarines were ideal and a hard-pressed attack must have succeeded. But they had been so shaken by their harrying both from the air and from the surface that only one U-boat ever reached the close screen and that was easily dealt with. The support group had a little sport in attacking two U-boats which we fixed by H/F D/F, but the convoy was never in danger. The Senior Officer of the group was most helpful and after the first incident suggested that, to save time, I should give his ships their orders direct instead of passing requests first to him. The two groups worked splendidly together.

Just before dawn I did the same ninety-degree turn to starboard and again the plan worked well. We were then able to direct aircraft on to submarines which had surfaced and were reporting that they had missed us, and as a result the first Liberator from Iceland made several attacks. That day was very like the last, except that the pack did not press in nearly so close and the weather was deteriorating steadily, with a strong southeasterly wind which reduced the speed of the convoy considerably. The visibility remained good, however, and we were able to home the aircraft on to many targets, and the ships of the convoy spent most of the day carrying out emergency turns to avoid danger. They were manoeuvring beautifully now, and never before could any one convoy have made so many alterations of course. The result would not have shamed a battle fleet.

The escorts usually reached the spot where the submarine had been too late to pick it up on asdics, and although there were one or two reasonable attacks, mainly by ships of the support group, we got no more kills. There was one affair which might have proved most exciting. Late in the afternoon a Liberator signalled that he had attacked a submarine with his last depth charge and that the U-boat was circling on the surface apparently too damaged to dive. We shot after it at full speed with a heavy sea making us roll and yaw wildly. Again I knew the pilot and there was a good interchange of R/T in which we made some rather rude suggestions as to alternative weapons to drop. My gun crews were closed up and all was ready. Homing to the aircraft's signals, we soon sighted it circling on the horizon — the situation seemed too good to be true. It was. Shortly after, the Liberator reported 'U-boat dived', and we rejoined, furious at our luck for no time could be spared for a hunt.

That night was again quiet. It was some time in the early morning of 21st May that Admiral Doenitz called off the pack, for we saw no more submarines, despite first-class air cover, this time provided from Ireland by Liberators and Sunderlands.

Radio communication with aircraft had been excellent and they knew their job and worked well with us. Homing on to the convoy, too, worked splendidly and there were no 'Not mets'. It was all a pleasing contrast to the days of 1940 and 1941. There was only one slip-up, when one of the aircraft insisted, whenever he saw a U-boat, on making long sighting reports to his base in Iceland hundreds of miles away. This meant that when he was transmitting on W/T I could not raise him on R/T and wasted vital minutes before being able to give him urgent instructions. It was only after some extremely forthright personal conversation with the Captain of the aircraft, during which I pointed out that it was the escort that wanted information and not his base, who could do nothing about it anyway, that the situation became satisfactory.

On 22nd May an easterly gale was blowing, the enemy had left, and I dispatched the support group to go off to another convoy.

The next task was the battle of the reports and, helped by improving weather, we all set to with a will. The day before arrival, I steamed round the screen and collected the lot, so that before we berthed in Londonderry the complete report, typed and signed, was ready for dispatch.

Both the Commodore and I kept our London engagements without difficulty, but my honeymoon was regrettably short, for the group sailed again within ten days of arrival.

My discussions with the Germans showed that this pack, which consisted of four groups, totalling over twenty boats, and was the last to attack a convoy that summer, only claimed to have fired one torpedo; U-594, 258, 209, 273 and 381 were sunk and those lost included Admiral Doenitz's son, while in addition two U-boats were damaged.

It was interesting, later, to talk to German Captains and to analyse the thoughts of the U-boats who took part in attacks on B 7 Group during those ten weeks between mid-March and the end of May. I do not think that any submarine attacked all three convoys, but many of them had two smacks at us and of those sunk at least two were attacking our convoys for the second time. If they listened to our R/T, as some of them did, they must have got very tired of our voices!

With a score of fifteen U-boats sunk and six seriously damaged, against sixteen ships lost in the three convoys, the result was even better than we guessed at the time. This justified the hard work of B 7 Group, and of the aircraft and of the support groups also responsible.

Doenitz gives us an unsolicited testimonial in his book, when he says:

The overwhelming superiority achieved by the enemy defence was finally proved beyond dispute in the operations against convoys SC 130 and HX 239. The convoy escorts worked in exemplary harmony with the specially trained support groups. To that must be added the continuous air cover which was provided by the carrier-borne [for HX 239] and long-range shore-based aircraft, most of them equipped with the new radar... Operations could only be resumed if we succeeded in radically increasing the fighting power of the U-boats.

This was the logical conclusion to which I came, and accordingly I withdrew the boats from the North Atlantic. On 24th May I ordered them to proceed, using the utmost caution, to the area south-west of the Azores. We had lost the Battle of the Atlantic.

As Captain Roskill puts it in his official summing up:

The battle never again reached the same pitch of intensity nor hung so delicately in the balance, as during the spring of 1943. It is therefore fair to claim that the victory here recounted marked one of the decisive stages of the war; for the enemy made his greatest effort against our Atlantic life-line and he failed. After forty-five months of unceasing battle, of a more exacting and arduous nature than posterity may easily realize, our convoy escorts and aircraft had won the triumph they so richly merited.

13. SUPPORTING

As at the end of May 1943 Doenitz withdrew his submarines from the North Atlantic — except for one or two who were left to report the weather — our life became rather dull. The enemy maintained a continual stream of propaganda, however, threatening the wrath to come, and we imagined that he was keeping his training flotillas busy producing fresh crews and the dockyards hard at work fitting more anti-aircraft guns on the U-boats. There was also much talk about secret weapons and new tactics.

The group had four and a half months of monotonous running across the Western Ocean unrelieved by any excitement, except for the first passage in early June when we helped 'fix' a weather reporter which was smartly sunk by the 1st Escort Group which was supporting our convoy, and except for the last passage with SC 142 in early October when we ran across a U-boat on its way to convoy ON 202, which was being heavily attacked to the north of us by U-boats armed with the first acoustic torpedoes. I am afraid on this occasion we failed to make a kill, although we surprised the U-boat.

Life at Londonderry continued to be pleasant. We returned after one trip to find that a remarkable coincidence had occurred, for Wren Gretton and Steward Harvey had both been advanced to the leading rate, and their 'hooks', as the new badges of rank were called, had to be properly celebrated.

I did a great deal of lobbying in order that we should become a support group, which was a much more interesting task than the routine work of a normal convoy escort. Although we had four corvettes in the group which were a little slow for the supporting role, I still thought that we could do better than most, and we were very much on the crest of the wave after the successes of April and May. But my pleas remained unheard until the middle of October 1943, when we were allowed the privilege of one run as a support group. But it was no ordinary period and we were lucky enough to have few dull moments during the twenty-five days which we spent at sea.

The start was not promising, for the *Duncan* developed serious leaks in the main steam valves when warming through the engines before sailing and could not take part in the pre-convoy exercises. I went in the *Vidette* instead and we had a busy few days, as we had now firm information on the new enemy weapons, and we were trying out various dodges to defeat them.

The acoustic torpedoes had the disagreeable habit of listening for your propellers and then homing on the noise; neatly blowing off your stern when they hit.

They were anti-escort weapons and proved effective, but they were not so devastating as they at first seemed. For one thing, they could not 'hear' you if you went slowly. For another, the noise from their own propellers interfered if they went fast, so they were very slow torpedoes and fast ships could get away from them. Their 'ears' too had a certain maximum range. So, what with one thing and another, we had some tricks to defeat them, which in fact we did. The Admiralty had also produced a contraption — the 'Foxer' — which ships not having the speed to escape could tow astern. It made a great clanging noise and was supposed to attract the torpedo, which then missed the ship. Unfortunately, although it was effective, it made the asdic practically useless and I never streamed it in the *Duncan*, though some of the slower ships found it very useful from time to time.

After the exercise I returned to the anchorage to find the *Duncan* ready for sea and transferred back to her to wait the few hours we had before final sailing.

I was lucky to have a First Lieutenant who was quite capable of running the ship at sea or in harbour when I was not aboard. Only in this way would our custom of continuing to command one's own ship in addition to the escort group have worked, as the escort commander must be free to transfer to other ships when necessary, either for operational or for exercise reasons.

The Americans, with their logical minds, do not use our system and have a Senior Officer in the 'Flagship' of each group or squadron, in addition to the Captain of the Flagship. The advantages of our system are intangible — the avoidance of friction due to the presence in a small ship both of a Group Commander and the Captain; the satisfaction of continuing to command one's own ship; or the closer personal touch one has with officers and men. Whatever reason was the right one, however, I know that I produced the best results when I was also Captain of my own ship, and I also had the experience of carrying a Senior Officer in my own ship and later of being Senior Officer in someone's else's ship, as well as doing both jobs simultaneously. Given a reliable First Lieutenant, I prefer our system every time, though the other, by logic, appears the better.

The wind was blowing very hard, but the ship seemed reasonably steady and I went aft to my harbour cabin to read the mass of paper which seemed always to be dumped on board at the last minute. By a happy chance the Tactical Unit happened to have sent one of its staff down river with some corrections to books, signal publications, and memoranda of every sort, which were mostly of little moment but which had to be read lest something important was missed. So she and I settled down to wade through them.

In the course of reading I happened to glance out of the cabin scuttle and noticed, to my horror, that the ship was dragging fast. I rushed up to the bridge, warning en route the Chief Engine Room Artificer, who was fortunately standing in the engine-room hatch, to stand by the throttles. An atmosphere of perfect calm was prevailing at the compass. A very green pair of officers on anchor watch had failed to notice anything amiss and, when I arrived, they were diligently taking bearings on a distant mountain, while a few yards off the port beam the rocks were racing past. A few moments later the wind and tide caught the ship and thrust her broadside on to MacKinney's Light, one of the large wooden beacons which marked the edge of the channel. There was a loud rending sound, the beacon toppled slowly over, and its timber floated away down the river. By then there was nothing to do but slip the cable and hope to get out stern first because, according to the chart, our bows should be already aground. But the ship, fortunately, had not yet touched and we managed to emerge intact, except for the anchor and eight shackles of cable which had been buoyed for easy recovery.

We were due to sail in half an hour's time, so a carefully worded signal was sent off to the Senior Officer ashore who, luckily, had a strong sense of humour in addition to being extremely helpful to his ships and, being eighteen miles up the river, would not yet have heard the news. The Tactical Unit's representative stepped smartly aboard a NAAFI launch which arrived at the critical moment and we steamed thankfully out to sea, secure in the knowledge that much would be forgotten by the time we returned.

Time has dimmed my memory and I have told the story so often that perhaps the signal has improved in repetition, but I like to think that it read, 'Regret to report that my starboard anchor and eight shackles of cable will be found, buoyed, 340° 4 cables from where MacKinney's Beacon used to be.' On our return four weeks later we secured alongside and, without warning, a lighter quietly approached, our anchor and cable were hauled inboard, and we heard no more of this regrettable affair.

The group consisted of well-tried ships but there were only five of them, for both the *Tay* and the *Snowflake* were refitting. Next day, 13th October, we caught up our convoy, ON 206, escorted by B 6 Group which was made up mainly of Norwegian ships. They were a grand crowd, with whom it was easy to work and, what is more, I had managed to meet the Senior Officer in the *Fame* just before sailing, and we were able to work out some plans. We agreed to separate our groups into two divisions, the fast and the slow, irrespective of which group they belonged to, and the slow ships remained with the close escort and the fast came with me and hared around the convoy to discourage U-boats approaching.

There was no doubt that whether it concerned the direction of the convoy, the escorting aircraft, or other groups which were supporting, the Commander of the close escort must exercise tactical command, whatever his rank. He usually had the best facilities, he was in the closest touch with the Commodore and he was with the convoy throughout the passage and so provided the continuity of experience which a support group lacked. This problem raised much controversy, but having carried out the roles of close escort commander, support group commander, and having flown often in escorting aircraft, I am convinced that it was the only answer.

The convoy had been sighted by the enemy before we arrived, and a small pack had succeeded in assembling before the aircraft had had time to come out to deal with them. We had a busy night attacking one submarine which had been detected by the *Vanquisher*, one of the destroyers of B 6 Group, but this was the only one which got close to the convoy. We did not succeed in killing it, for its Captain was a wily man who knew the tricks of the trade, but we kept him down until dawn and then we both left the spot at high speed to rejoin.

Two Liberators were with the convoy at first light on 14th October and the next thing we heard, while we were still seventeen miles astern of the convoy, was a report from one of them, 'Am attacking U-boat on port beam of convoy'. The *Duncan* turned at once towards him and made every effort to close as soon as possible, leaving the *Vanquisher* to follow astern. Next came another signal that one aircraft had been hard hit and that a second had taken over the attack. Then we saw a Liberator flying back towards the convoy with an engine on fire, and soon afterwards the second plane was sighted ahead of us dropping depth-charges. Both aircraft had made gallant runs in the face of heavy flak, and after a third attack the U-boat dived. The first aircraft had to 'ditch' near the convoy, most of the crew being picked up by the *Pink*, and the second, also with one engine out of action as a result of flak, made certain we had sighted his smoke marker and then started back for his base, many hundred miles away. His cheerful signals in this alarming situation were most inspiring and we were delighted later to hear that he had got back safely.

Doenitz had ordered his U-boats to 'fight' their way through to the convoy with the anti-aircraft gun, and the aircraft were having a bad time, but they were sinking submarines.

After an unsuccessful search both ships returned towards the convoy which by now had many submarines in contact, and I think it unlikely that our U-boat got home undamaged. The fun of supporting instead of acting as a close escort was that there was no need to stay rigidly with the convoy; ships had freedom to roam about looking for trouble and we usually managed to find it, whereas on close escort duty there was never time to do more than a quick counter-attack and then rejoin.

The rest of the day was spent chasing around the convoy in rather bad weather, investigating H/F D/F bearings and generally harrying the pack. Not long before dark an aircraft sent out the welcome signal, 'Have attacked U-boat, survivors in the water', and we shot off to investigate, followed this time by the *Vidette*. The position given was much closer to the convoy than was actually the case, and it was after dark before we reached the spot, having homed on to the aircraft's radio signals. But flares showed the position of the sinking and we were soon steaming through shouting men. It was not easy to decide what to do. There were other U-boats about which were well capable of torpedoing a ship which was stopped. The *Vidette*, feeling her years and lack of a third boiler, was some miles astern, and to make matters worse the men in the water had not kept together and were scattered over several miles. We were a long way from the convoy, which needed our support. And there was little time to spare.

As soon as the *Vidette* arrived we stopped and lowered a whaler in the middle of a bunch of men. The first two hauled in were dead, for the Atlantic in winter is very cold, and the remainder were so exhausted that there were long delays. Then the escort commander asked us to get back as soon as possible as there were many submarines in contact, so the whaler was hoisted and both ships set course to rejoin at full speed. Three minutes after regaining our station on the extended screen the radar operator detected a submarine coming in on the surface from ahead. It was a relief to the conscience that our early return had proved so necessary, because we had only picked up two men. We fired star shell, forced the U-boat to dive, and then started our 'anti-acoustic-torpedo tactics', which interfered seriously with the efficiency of our attack. The submarine was tough and experienced and we did not have time to make certain of a kill. The *Vidette* and I stayed over it for a couple of hours and then rejoined, while several more attacks were fended off by other escorts. The final blow to the enemy's efforts to get into the convoy came at dawn, when again we picked up a submarine on our radar and again forced it to dive and attacked it, without any promising result.

Several days of attack had resulted in no damage to the convoy or escorts, and our first encounter had proved most satisfactory.

The last two days having been heavy on oil, we started to fuel from the tanker *Roxane*, which was the immediate signal for a rapid deterioration in the weather. I have fuelled at sea on countless occasions but this was far and away the worst. The men working on the foc'sle were drenched by spray and once knocked over by waves. The ship was rolling heavily and I succeeded in parting one large hawser and with it the hose. Oil from the burst hose made work on deck even more dangerous, but after six miserable hours we managed to top up complete.

Half-way through this operation, the group was told to leave this convoy and go to another, ONS 20, which was being heavily attacked astern. So the rest of the group parted company at once, and I arranged to catch them up after I had completed oiling.

I then got the opportunity to talk to the two prisoners, who had recovered from their immersion and were being employed on ship cleaning. They seemed quite happy and obviously appreciated the friendliness of the sailors with whom they were messed. We learned that the submarine was U-470, on its first operational trip; that the Captain, who had been lost, was in his first command and that he had once been the radio officer in the *Altmark*. The aircraft depth-charge attacks had been very accurate and none of the twelve charges were more than thirty yards away. I also confirmed for the first time what had long been suspected, that some U-boats listened to our R/T conversations and appeared to gain much value from them.

We joined up with the rest of the group just before dark and after spreading the ships out into their cruising formation I went below for a short sleep — six hours fuelling was very exhausting. I had not been down long before the First Lieutenant reported from the bridge, '*Sunflower*'s got one,' and a signal followed to say that she had detected a U-boat, had dropped depth-charges on it only a few seconds after it had dived, and had blown it to the surface again. She had first sighted the boat at 700 yards range, it had only dived 300 yards away and she had seen the conning tower emerging out of the depth-charge pattern. The *Sunflower* turned to deliver a second attack, the U-boat got down again just in time, and the second pattern also seemed very accurate.

The *Sunflower*'s depth-charge crews had done great work in difficult conditions. The seas were rough, and as the ship turned, waves came sweeping down her waist, knocking over men reloading the charges and washing them along the deck. One man was knocked out and several others had broken bones; but they reloaded all the throwers, except one, in time for the second attack. We searched the sea thoroughly for several hours but no trace was found of the boat except much oil on the surface of the water. We learned afterwards that U-631 had been sunk.

The group were in the track of the next convoy and shortly after giving up the search, the ships came bearing down upon us. As had been feared there were mistakes in recognition, for each side thought the other was a U-boat and before we knew quite what had happened, the sky was filled with bursting star shell. Luckily no shots were fired, but we were afraid that the firework display would silhouette the convoy to the formidable pack which had been following it for two days. Strange to relate, however, it had the reverse effect and scared them away, for no more attacks were made that night and I reckon the Germans thought that it was a deliberate diversion to draw them off.

The weather was still bad and next morning, 18th October, I had considerable difficulty in exchanging papers and gossip with the Escort Commander who was in the *Bentinck*, an American-built destroyer escort, which was rolling very heavily. After apologizing for the scenes of the previous night, I set off with the *Vidette* and spent a miserable day searching around the convoy in shocking weather, leaving the three corvettes on the close screen. That night the *Vanquisher* joined us from convoy ON 206, but nothing was seen until the next morning when she detected and attacked a submarine well astern of the convoy. This was the last one to appear, and it was then clear that the pack had been called off, so the *Pink* was detached to Newfoundland to land her injured airmen, for by this time we were close off the Grand Banks.

Then we fuelled again, and having also collected some depth charges from the convoy, we left before dark to meet our next commitment, ON 207, which was still some way to the eastward. The two days of passage were a welcome rest period after a tiring week. We were in excellent heart and keen for some sport, and again there was not long to wait.

ON 207 had an extremely strong escort. Operating inside the convoy was an escort carrier, the *Biter*, and in addition to the close escort, Captain Walker's famous support group, EG 2, was also in company, though it was out of sight to the southward. We closed the convoy and, having collected the necessary information, were given a station a hundred miles to the north-north-west, which we reached early on 23rd October.

The next alarm came rather unexpectedly. The *Sunflower* had a defective radar set, the spare part for which was not carried by any ship in the group, so a signal had been sent off requesting that the part should be flown out to us. Our good liaison with 15 Group ensured success, and one of the aircraft due to escort the convoy was diverted slightly to drop us the spare part. About half an hour before he was due over us the Captain of the aircraft signalled that he was attacking a submarine. We altered course to join him at full speed and arrived in time to see the splash of his explosions on the horizon! The pilot had left the intercommunication system switched into the radio-telephone, and we could hear everything that was said in the aircraft. It was just like listening to a broadcast of a bomber over Berlin, but even more realistic, for the crew did not know that they could be heard in the ships. 'The ——'s going down, bomb doors open,' came clearly over the air and the Captain's remarks when he missed were worth going miles to hear.

The *Duncan* and the *Vidette* were soon at the scene, to be followed later by the corvettes, led by the *Loosestrife* who had well exceeded her designed speed during the chase. We soon passed the smoke float, which the aircraft had dropped to mark her attack, without picking up the submarine, and then I spread the five ships and started a search initially in the direction of the convoy. We were lucky to detect it within half an hour. I missed with my first 'hedgehog' shot, but the second one got three hits and, after some long minutes, gruesome evidence of the destruction of U-274 began to rise to the surface. It had been a very exciting hunt in the cat-and-mouse tradition for we were using slow speed and we stopped every now and then to make quite certain of the course and the speed of the submarine.

We were particularly pleased to get a most apt and friendly biblical signal over the air from Captain Walker, for he had not bagged one that particular trip yet and we were delighted to have wiped the eye for once of the leading expert in the navy, who had forgotten more about 'pinging' than any of us had ever learnt.

After continuing to support this convoy for a day or two without further incident, we closed and fuelled again, leaving on 25th October to meet ON 208, which was also west-bound. At first it seemed that ON 208 would provide no sport and after a blank day or two we topped up with fuel and left to meet an east-bound convoy HX 263. This, we hoped, would be our last job, for three weeks of consistently bad weather had already passed — a long time in a small ship in the North Atlantic winter.

But our luck held, and only six hours after leaving ON 208, the *Vidette* detected a U-boat following in the track of the convoy which, after a long hunt, the *Sunflower* succeeded in sinking with a good 'hedgehog' attack. The trophies collected were even more gruesome and more numerous than in the last attack and the *Sunflower* had reaped the fruit of much hard training. I was particularly pleased with this affair because in order to sweep down the wake of the convoy I had deliberately disregarded my orders and diverted from the route given me by headquarters.

There is little more to tell. We met HX 263 in filthy weather off the Newfoundland Banks on 31st October and supported it for several days without incident. We were running short of food — except for bread and corned beef — and the *Pink*, which had been to Newfoundland to land the injured aircrew, provided some welcome potatoes which she towed astern for us to pick up in turn. The *Sunflower* nearly ran out of lubricating oil, so some drums were floated over to keep her going and the *Loosestrife* fuelled in the roughest weather I have ever seen. But these are only domestic details. At last the signal to leave the convoy was received, and we gained our release from what was becoming a very tedious business.

In the *Duncan* we had steamed 6,700 miles, we had crossed the Atlantic five times, we had fuelled at sea on six occasions, and we had also topped up with depth-charges. On 5th November the group sailed up the River Foyle feeling very pleased with itself. The track chart of our wanderings resembled the antics of a fly drying after a dip in a bottle of ink.

The group had kept going remarkably well and all the radar and asdic sets were working on return to harbour, except for the *Loosestrife* whose anti-submarine dome had been ripped off by heavy seas. There had been no engine defects and we had proved that if B 7 were given a run 'supporting', we could make a good job of it. We had managed to sink three U-boats without loss in the convoys we supported and we wanted to have another run at this entertaining sport.

But it was not to be, and we returned at once to the same old round of Londonderry to Newfoundland and back again.

We were to have no more battles and remarkably few incidents, though we did succeed in sailing once or twice with an escort carrier in company and I have a note in my game book, 'Handed U-666 on a plate to H.M.S. *Fencer* in February 1944,' but I can remember very little of the affair.

We also sailed several times with 'Mac' ships, which were tankers or grain carriers fitted with flight decks and, in the case of the grain ships, with a hangar as well. These ships operated two or three Swordfish aircraft in addition to their normal role of carrying cargo. The Master and crew came from the Merchant Service with a small naval party to fly and maintain the aircraft, and this unusual arrangement worked admirably, and the Swordfish flew many long hours and did much useful work. The Master, after a week's course at the Western Approaches Tactical Unit under Captain Roberts, where he learned about the theory of operating aircraft in support of convoys, and after a short indoctrination into the aircraft business, was soon off to sea with a naval aviator as his adviser. One got the impression of keenness and quiet efficiency and it was sad that, by the time the Mac ships had started to operate, the main Atlantic battle had been won, and they were given few opportunities of getting at submarines.

I always remember one Mac ship which had flown off a Swordfish to look for a submarine fixed by the H/F D/F set. The weather became unexpectedly very bad during the sortie and, when the aircraft was recalled, there was a full southwesterly gale blowing up the stern of the convoy, which was steering north-east. To have turned the ship into the wind to land on would have been too dangerous in such weather, so we arranged for the Swordfish to come in over the bow, instead of the normal method over the stern, and he made a splendid landing!

Alas! the Mac ship rolled heavily just after the aircraft had touched down and he slipped gently over the side into the sea. But the *Vidette*, which was standing by, picked up the crew with little difficulty and they had a rather uncomfortable passage back to the U.K.

In December 1943 the *Duncan* had to return to a dockyard for a further major refit despite the fact that she had only left Tilbury in April, after many months under repair. She leaked everywhere and the boiler-and engine-rooms were both death traps, for oily water splashed about the bilges and the deck plates were always slippery. We had to dock at Argentia after one passage to patch up some big splits in the ship's side abreast the foremost funnel, and the U.S. Navy, on completion of the repairs, told me that she was quite unfit for sea!

During every trip we swore 'never again' and promised to write a strong report on return to harbour. When we arrived at Londonderry it always seemed different, and after a bath and a glass of sherry, opinion would quickly turn to 'let us try one more trip', and the letter would never be written!

Eventually I broke wireless silence in the middle of the Atlantic and reported that we must be docked on arrival. The ship was promptly withdrawn from service.

Later, in early 1944, when I was embarked in the frigate *Chelmer*, the group succeeded in finding a submarine which was clearly most experienced. It dived to about 700 feet where we seemed quite unable to do it any harm, despite the use of all the latest 'Johnny Walker' ideas for 'plaster' attacks. Fortunately C 2 Group were in the vicinity on a support job and we handed over the submarine to them, together with a couple of Castle-class corvettes, which were doing their first trip with the group and which had been fitted with a new anti-submarine weapon, the 'Squid'. C 2 Group succeeded in sinking U-744, but I am afraid we had little to do with this successful conclusion, and anyhow my recollections of this affair are rather dim, for on the west-bound passage I had gone down with a mild bout of typhoid fever and had been carried aboard the *Chelmer* in a stretcher at Argentia, just before sailing eastbound. I did not take over command until the day before we picked up the U-boat and I am not especially proud of my performance.

After another trip across the ocean, this time in the *Vidette*, it became increasingly clear that it was time to go ashore for a spell. The group was being disbanded as part of the programme of preparation for the invasion of France, so I did not mind leaving and could not face the thought of starting out again with a crowd of complete strangers.

After an excellent long leave in the glorious weather of the spring of 1944, my intrigues to get command of an anti-submarine escort-carrier failed, and I was condemned to three months' book-writing in the Admiralty — on a new set of escort of convoy instructions — and then placed firmly in the basement of the Cabinet Office, where I remained for the rest of the war.

I escaped only for one glorious week, soon after the surrender of Germany, when I flew to Flensburg, Kiel and Bergen in a Coastal Command aircraft, with Captain Gilbert Roberts and Wing Commander Gates, to have a look at the surrendered submarines and talk to their Commanders.

14. THOUGHTS IN RETROSPECT

IT had been a fascinating experience to visit the U-boat headquarters in Germany and Norway and one came away with a tremendous regard for the courage and determination of the Germans, but also with surprise at their lack of ultimate success. Their morale and discipline in defeat was very high. Although they had lost over 1,000 U-boats since the start of the war — 780 by enemy action and 220 by scuttling — and although over 32,000 officers and men were lost — a very high proportion of the total force — they were full of confidence in the new, fast types of U-boats which were just beginning to come into action in quantity. I very well remember listening to one of the experienced Captains describing with tears in his eyes how he had the cruiser *Birmingham* in the sights of his new Mark 21 U-boat only a few hours after the surrender.

I left Flensburg with a far lower opinion of the German naval scientific effort than I had expected. During the war I had always thought that they were ahead of us. I remembered the acoustic torpedo, the *Lut* or circling torpedo, the remote-controlled glider bomb, the bubble asdic decoy and the 'Snort', none of which we possessed and all of which seemed to catch us bending, though, in the case of the acoustic torpedo, not for long. Yet when one heard of the German torpedo failures, of the delays in getting the new and advanced methods of propulsion to sea, and of the fearful mistakes which their scientists made over radar and radar counter measures, one realized that our 'boffins' had been a great deal better than we thought at the time!

My time in B 7 Group had been happy throughout — I was very lucky in the Captains, and their ships without exception followed their lead. Each one was good in a different way. The *Vidette* was efficient, cheerful and always ready for anything new. The *Sunflower* was splendid, and her Canadian Captain had an inquiring and keen mind which tackled problems in an unconventional way and much helped me, with my traditional approach. The *Loosestrife*, once the new Captain had joined, was always steady and she had the best communications team in the group. Her Leading Telegraphist was outstanding, and could always be depended on to pick up any signals on the air. The *Snowflake*, with her Australian Captain who had a highly developed sense of humour, was first class in every way. *Pink* took life rather seriously and it was some time before he got used to the stream of abuse which used to pour from my bridge when anything was happening. But his ship worked very well and he was a most competent fighting seaman. The *Alisma* was only with us for one battle, during which she did magnificently. She had an Australian Captain and officers with a crew from the Royal Navy, and she ran very well. The *Tay* I knew better than any. She improved fast and ended up as a most efficient ship with a cheerful wardroom. And, of course, her Captain has well earned his niche in naval history.

In the *Duncan*, I had a grand crowd of officers and men and the First Lieutenant, who in addition to being able to take charge of the ship if I happened to be away in another member of the group, had the equivalent of 'green fingers' with electronic gear. He had a wonderful way with broken asdic sets or radars, and as a result I was able to let my A/S Bosun and my radar officer roam around the ships of the group in turn, being confident that my own sets would always perform well.

Some time after I left the Western Approaches Command, I had the pleasure of circulating to all ships a copy of Commodore D Londonderry's remarks on B 7 Group's last passage in March 1944:

> Thus ends the uneventful passage of B 7 Group's last convoy operation. I consider it fortunate that providence has dictated that the enemy should so frequently have attacked convoys escorted by B 7, who have consistently beaten off all attacks and inflicted severe damage on the enemy, in particular, the prolonged battle fought in the early days of May 1943.
>
> Nevertheless, I consider it should be put on record that B 7, as a close escort group, has distinguished itself not only by sinking U-boats but the more unspectacular but equally important duty of protecting the convoys for whom it was responsible.

It is now some twenty years after the major battles which I have described in the last few chapters, and with the help of the official histories, both British and American, of Admiral Doenitz's memoirs, of numerous other books and of much discussion, it is possible to ruminate on what happened and to derive some wiser conclusions than those made nearer the time. None of my points are original, but perhaps they bear repetition.

Sir Winston Churchill was never in any doubt as to the grave danger to the Allied cause from U-boat attack in the Battle of the Atlantic. He took a keen personal interest in the day-to-day detail of the battle, he took the chair at meetings of the Cabinet Committee set up to direct the national effort at sea, and he made sure that our Allies across the Atlantic were fully aware of the critical importance of the outcome. In his *History of the Second World War*, Sir Winston confesses that the only thing which really frightened him was the U-boat peril.

Yet in the navy we started the war insufficiently prepared, and our priorities for ships, aircraft and weapons were wrong. Trade protection, as I have said earlier, was looked upon as a rather unfashionable activity to be left to the dug-outs, the reserves, and those regulars not good enough for the 'Fleet'. This attitude was responsible for many unnecessary losses in the earlier years of the war. Fortunately for us, despite the efforts of Doenitz, the German Naval Command made the same mistakes, while Hitler and the High Command (the O.K.W.) had not, until too late, the remotest conception of the importance of the Atlantic War and of the U-boat arm in particular. Nor did the German Air Force ever really understand what important service they could render to the U-boats. Interservice rivalry was more important than the common cause.

There is every reason to believe that our potential enemies of today have a keen and accurate appreciation of maritime warfare, and we must ensure that we have enough merchant ships to sustain this island both in peace and war, and the ships and aircraft to protect them.

The second point which now strikes me forcibly is the need to design our warships, aircraft and weapons for a tough war in all climates and to try them out in realistic tests in peace in every kind of weather. In World War I, our shells had been no good; but in World War II, we remembered this, and our explosives were on the whole satisfactory, though some of the bombs were bad. Our torpedoes were elderly but well tried and reliable — both the Germans and the Americans started the war with advanced but useless torpedoes! The design of our main propulsion machinery was also rather ancient, but both engines and boilers were rugged and reliable and ran like trains throughout the war. The Germans introduced some sophisticated high-pressure, high-temperature machinery just before the war started, and they had many teething troubles which resulted in ships being out of action for months at a time. The lesson here is to avoid getting new equipment into full production until it has been thoroughly tested at sea.

But after re-reading the reports of some of my group's battles in the dispassionate light of twenty years after, I cannot help thinking that we had too many material failures. Asdics out of action or not fully working; radar out of action; failure to fire depth-charges or firing incomplete patterns at the wrong depth; mistakes with the 'hedgehog'; failure in communication and failure to illuminate when required. All ships reported one or more examples of these types. Yet we never missed a chance to exercise and we were a well-trained group with an above-average standard of maintenance. Without seeking excuses, I believe that if the designers of the equipment had appreciated that most of the ship and its gear would be drenched with salt water for weeks on end, there would have been far less trouble. Moreover, ships were immobilized in really cold weather due to ice and were uninhabitable in really hot weather. A crash programme of 'Arcticization' was necessary, which took precious ships from operations for long periods.

And, finally, on material matters, the arrangements for resisting and then dealing with action damage due to shells, bombs, mines or torpedoes were inadequate, and many ships were lost unnecessarily in the early years of the war. A Damage Control School had to be set up to evolve better protection and methods, and to train officers and men in the art.

All this may sound critical, but it is constructive criticism, and other navies made the same or worse mistakes. But we must not repeat our mistakes again, for the lessons had all been learnt in the hard way during World War One and promptly forgotten in the peace. I believe that our fleet training between the wars was very good, although not always directed to the most important roles; and I am certain that no other navy could have produced the Captains of the fleet destroyers which took part in the Norwegian campaign, in the operations at Dunkirk, Greece and Crete, and in the Mediterranean and Arctic convoys, and came up smiling after each action, ready and eager for more.

Today there are plenty of exercises with convoys and shipping, and the weather is not allowed to curtail the exercises too much. But bad weather is expensive in damage and it is tempting to cut things short when the gales start. The temptation must be resisted!

My next key point concerns the value of aircraft over the sea, which I have already stressed so often. Whether fixed or rotary winged, these machines are an integral part of a modern navy, and no ship can survive in a war against an up-to-date enemy without their help. That is why the navy must keep so close to Coastal Command, and why some form of ship to carry aircraft will always be needed. One can argue all day about the size of aircraft-carriers, and quote the merits of vertical take-off and other modern devices which can affect the size of the carrier. But ships cannot survive without aircraft, and shore air-bases cannot provide all the necessary protection.

As to the effect of the aircraft on the Battle of the Atlantic, at risk of repetition, co-operation with aircraft was the key to success. Directly an aircraft joined the escort of a shadowed convoy, the radio traffic from the U-boats dried up in a magical fashion, and it is a fact that less than a dozen ships were lost in daylight in convoys which were escorted by aircraft as well as surface ships. This co-operation depended on three factors: a close understanding of each other's problems, reliable and quick communication, and good joint training.

We had little trouble with naval aircraft whose crews' training was similar to ours; moreover, after 1941, the Swordfish had an excellent R/T set which invariably gave 'loud and clear' communication. At the start of the war, and indeed until the early stages of 1942, this was not true of the Coastal Command aircraft. The crews were desperately keen and very brave, but they had not been trained correctly, they did not understand the Escort Commander's problem, and they resented having to place themselves under his orders. Navigation was not good, convoys were often miles out of position and aircraft often failed to find them after hours of searching, or else arrived with little fuel remaining. Only when radio-homing procedure had been introduced did the percentage of 'Not mets' reduce.

By 1943, with Sir John Slessor at Coastal Command and Air Marshal Slatter in 15 Group Headquarters at Derby House, Liverpool, the atmosphere had changed completely. The crews were splendidly trained, co-operation with the surface escorts was good, and the results speak for themselves. In fact, 120 Squadron, with very-long-range Liberators working from Iceland, was the finest anti-submarine squadron in the world in 1943.

All my staff and many of the officers of the group used to fly in Coastal Command aircraft on operational flights, and I managed myself to log over one hundred operational flying hours with Coastal Command. We took Royal Air Force officers to sea during exercises and sometimes on operations and we held post-mortem meetings either at Londonderry or at the airfield most concerned, after all convoys of interest. In this way we got to know the Captains of aircraft and broke down the barriers between us.

I yield to no one in my admiration of the performance of Coastal Command from early 1943 until the end of the war. It was magnificent. Nevertheless, owing to the inadequate weapons provided to both R.A.F. and F.A.A. aircraft and to the lack of training previously described, early results were very disappointing. Despite published claims, it is a fact that only one German submarine was sunk by the unaided effort of aircraft of Coastal Command or of the Fleet Air Arm from the start of the war until August 1941, and this was killed at anchor by the *Warspite*'s Swordfish at the second battle of Narvik. After that date, kills quickly increased until in 1943 success became the order of the day. But this should not have taken three years of war and millions of tons of lost shipping to achieve.

And one final thought stems from my visit to Flensburg in May 1945 and much subsequent study of the 'Walter' U-boats, one or two of which only had been produced by the end of the war and which we found scuttled in the Baltic.

These craft were true submarines and could remain submerged for long periods and also steam at high speed under water — twenty-five knots was claimed for the Type 26. They were the forerunners of the nuclear-propelled submarines which are now revolutionizing naval warfare.

The 'Snort', or air breathing apparatus, which the Germans got out in late 1944 (and which is not mentioned, consequently, in my narrative) enabled the U-boats to remain safely at sea for long periods, and their losses dropped spectacularly when the 'Snort' had been widely fitted. But the U-boats' speed was low, they could not keep contact with convoys with air cover and they were still ineffective weapons.

Thus, although a true submarine with a high sustained submerged speed — the Walter boat — was just operational at the end of the war, development had gone in fits and starts. Hitler would authorize progress and then Goering would get the order cancelled owing to the shortage of the hydrogen-peroxide fuel required for his rockets. Hitler would again be persuaded to approve high priority and then Speer was unimpressed and refused the steel needed for the boats.

Fortunately for us, it was a sorry tale of muddle, and I believe firmly that if the 'go ahead' had been given early in the war, accompanied by a high priority of men and materials, the Battle of the Atlantic would have taken a different turn.

15. CONVOY MANAGEMENT AND THE CONVOY SYSTEM

CONVOY MANAGEMENT

The tactics of the defence of convoys from submarine attack is an art which has received much study since the end of World War II, and which I have no intention of discussing here. It is as well, however, to remark that it is essential that Escort Commanders have flexible minds, as must the staff directing affairs ashore. During World War Two the struggle against submarines was a continual see-saw, with first the offence and then the defence on top, depending entirely on the introduction of new weapons and new ideas. The strategy and the tactics both in attack and protection, therefore, varied continually, and equally so will they vary in the future.

The 'management' of the convoy at sea has received, however, little attention, and here I speak more from the point of view of the Escort Commander than of the Commodore. In this connection, it is worthy of note that 'marine disaster' such as collision, grounding and weather damage caused over twenty-five per cent of all the ships lost during the war (though the size of such ships was generally smaller than average and so the percentage of tonnage so lost was less). In addition, a large number of ships received damage which necessitated long periods out of action for repairs. This figure, of course, includes ships sailing both independently and in convoy.

The majority of such losses and damage were quite unnecessary. Over one thousand ships were lost through collision and grounding alone, owing to a variety of reasons, perhaps the most important of which was undue insistence on not burning navigation lights and on maintaining radio silence. There were areas round the coast which, at certain periods of the war, were entirely safe from submarine or air attack, but which were highly dangerous navigationally. Yet ships battled on, darkened, without any navigation lights, and the collisions which occurred were inevitable. Similarly to break W/T silence to request a position when lost somewhere off the north-west coast of Scotland or Ireland would, again, at certain periods of the war, have been quite safe from the point of view of enemy attack and would have ensured the safety of ships from grounding, yet the rules were never relaxed. Let us hope again that this lesson will be remembered by future planners and that flexibility in the instructions will be allowed.

I have constantly harped on the weather in the North Atlantic, which sometimes makes heaving to necessary to avoid damaging or losing ships. To heave to a convoy requires moral courage, for it is usually extremely difficult, if not impossible, to keep the ships together. I found, however, that by making the signal on low-power radio, 'Heave to, keeping the wind on the bow', it was possible to keep the convoy together, for as the wind shifted, ships automatically adjusted their heading, whereas if an attempt were made to heave to on a definite course, alterations would constantly be required which in such weather conditions were impossible to pass by flags. The communications experts disapproved of my breaking radio silence but it was only necessary to make one signal, and I believed that the risk was well worth taking, for the danger from the sea was far greater than from the enemy. During the worst gales many of the ships, particularly those in ballast, became unmanageable. The visibility would drop to about half a mile and control was quite impossible. In any case, the enemy could do little about it if they did hear the signal.

Fog and ice were bad enough taken separately; together they were highly dangerous, as I have already shown. It is worth remembering that signalling by whistle, and station-keeping by means of fog buoys towed astern, is a perfectly adequate way of controlling a convoy in fog, but only if these evolutions have been well practised beforehand. To enter a fog without previous training would bring tales of defective sirens and fog-buoy wires rusted on their reels. Previous practice was essential.

In fact, everything had to be exercised at the beginning of every convoy passage, both by the escorts and by the ships of the convoy. It was necessary to see that the escort oiler had the correct gear and knew how to work it, the convoy must practise emergency turns together, much signalling both on R/T and by flags must be exercised and the 'Mac'[5] ship or aircraft-carrier must fly on and off inside her 'box' in the convoy. By 1941 signalling, both by flashing light and by flags, was very good — a fine effort by officers who had received comparatively little training in peacetime.

Merchant-ship Captains, like others, prefer to get their heads down on their cabin settee after lunch, and I found that to carry out exercises in the forenoon and to threaten a repetition in the afternoon if things did not go right was the finest way to ensure success.

There were many other problems of domestic detail to watch. No refuse must be ditched, as this would give away the track of a convoy. Smoke was dangerous for obvious reasons and must be discouraged. Lights at night were not so serious, and sometimes it was better to burn navigation lights and so avoid collisions than to keep darkened, for the U-boats could

---

[5] See later, where the 'Mac' ship is described.

hear you on their hydrophones at far greater distances than they could see a coloured light.

At the Tactical School at Derby House, Liverpool, and at the Tactical Unit at Londonderry, we often discussed the performance of the U-boat hydrophones, and it was taken into account in the 'games' we played on the tactical table. We knew well that the U-boats used the hydrophone to warn them when an escort was coming in to attack, and the information enabled them to take avoiding action. But I do not recollect that we ever realized how far they could 'hear' ships and convoys on their hydrophones, especially in good weather.

I think that the biggest surprise I got when reading the published accounts of the exploits of U-boat Commanders was to discover this ability to detect convoys by hydrophone at such long range. The official histories do not give the matter much emphasis, but in the German accounts the phrase 'dived to listen on hydrophones' comes up again and again.

Kretchmer writes, 'We should have been in the vicinity of the convoy for which we had been searching [but there was no sign of it]. I decided to dive to listen with the hydrophones and, sure enough, the apparatus gave a bearing.'

And Muetzelburgh, another ace, recounts how in March 1941, when searching for a convoy reported by the Radio Interception Service 'the noise of propellers was heard on the hydrophones. It resembled a dull, subterranean grinding noise.' The U-boat surfaced, the visibility was excellent, but nothing could be seen. Only after over an hour and a half's steaming in the direction of the noise was the top of a mast sighted over the horizon.

But when the convoy was being shadowed, or in a danger area, a light gave an aiming mark and was highly dangerous. I found that a few well-aimed rounds of machine-gun bullets quickly doused the offender. It is consoling to realize now what one did not at the time, that Section Thirty-one of the Articles of War, which form part of the Naval Discipline Act, allows the Commanding Officer of a convoy escort 'to compel obedience by force of arms, without being liable for any loss of life or property that may result from his using such force.'

The discipline of ships in convoy was not too good in the early stages but quickly improved, and during the last three years of the war vast convoys, sometimes containing well over a hundred ships, were steaming safely across the ocean. Officers quite untrained in the art were able to keep good station, sometimes in elderly coal burners pressed into service from the edge of the scrap-heap, and despite the fact that the ships all had different turning circles and speeds, and merchant ships are not designed to turn quickly. Ships, too, had often very little margin of speed to regain station if they did drop back.

I have also remarked on the vast size of these armadas and it is well also to remember that to alter the course of a convoy by wheeling, as opposed to emergency turns together, took a long time, which was not surprising if the size and shape of the convoys was appreciated. Many minutes were required before the signal was received by all ships; then the wheel could only be carried out in small stages of, say, fifteen degrees at a time — otherwise there was confusion and station-keeping became difficult. To change the formation of the convoy, for instance to reduce the front when approaching a narrow channel, took hours; and the difficulties and delays in joining sections from the various ports in the United Kingdom and linking them up into one large ocean convoy were formidable. The sections from the Firth of Forth, the Clyde and from Liverpool used to meet at 'Oversay', which lay in the area between the Hebrides,

North East Ireland and the Mull of Kintyre, and often it took over a day before a big convoy was comfortably settled down into station.

Even to count the number of ships present took time and was not easy, especially in bad visibility; radar helped but was not infallible. Reading through old reports of proceedings recently, I came across the following remark which illustrates admirably what we were up against: 'It was not possible to carry out any exercises with the convoy throughout the passage owing to the fact that when there was not a full gale blowing we were in a thick fog.'

There was little one could do about 'Rompers' or 'Runners' — ships which deliberately broke out of the convoy — except to signal them in as threatening language as possible. With stragglers it was different, and I often found that a depth charge explosion pretty close would galvanize the firemen into activity. But one had to be careful about that game, because one Greek ship on whom I tried it immediately abandoned ship under the impression that she had been torpedoed.

Damaged or broken-down ships presented a horrible problem. Should they be told to return to harbour alone, to abandon ship having opened the sea cocks, to abandon ship and then signal for tugs to come out to tow, or should one get an escort or the rescue tug — if one was present — to tow, or detach one of the group to escort the ship concerned back to harbour? It was a hard decision, and, moreover, to sink ships loaded with light or timber cargo, was extraordinarily difficult.

One's position *vis-à-vis* the Commodore of the convoy was an interesting one. The Commodore was responsible for the discipline, station-keeping, and general administration of the convoy and was the source from which the ships received their instructions at sea. The Commodores, who were

230

accommodated, together with a small signal staff, in a ship of the convoy, had no facilities for appreciating the enemy situation, for their communication facilities were very limited.

The Escort Commander, on the other hand, was in a much better position. By using the radio sets of all ships of the group he could listen out on many channels and gain much information; he had the use of H/F D/F and M/F D/F sets, he had radar and he had asdic, and he was therefore able to produce a clear picture of the tactical situation. It was inevitable, therefore, that he must be in charge and that he must decide, for instance, on alterations of course, on the speed of the convoy and on other vital matters, though, of course, these decisions were taken, whenever possible, after consultation with the Commodore. It was necessary, too, to use much discretion, for many of the Commodores were distinguished Admirals who were not used to taking orders from comparatively junior officers.

As with all professions, some convoy Commodores were better than others, but on the whole they were a splendid team. By the end of the war there seemed to be about an equal number of retired Admirals and Merchant Service Captains all of whom were 'Commodore R.N.R.s', and there was little to choose between them. The Merchant Service Captains, with years of experience of merchant ships behind them, usually knew more of the domestic administration of the convoy, but the Admirals were better in an emergency. It was an honourable and very dangerous method of passing the years of retirement. There were no really difficult problems in one's relationship with the Commodores and I wish I had been able to meet more of them at conferences instead of exchanging greetings through megaphones, for one never met the Commodores of east-bound convoys which started at New

York, Sydney N.S., or Halifax, and being based at Londonderry instead of Liverpool or Greenock, I was never able to attend the convoy conferences of west-bound convoys.

Finally, one should say that the routing authorities achieved on more than one occasion the seemingly impossible. Our Command Headquarters at Derby House was efficient, helpful and most highly regarded by everyone in the Command. Nevertheless, on no less than two occasions, the convoy which I was escorting found itself meeting another convoy head on in mid-Atlantic. The first time was in daylight, but in filthy visibility and before the days of radar. The convoys were on exactly opposite courses and carried out a neat 'gridiron' without casualties. The second time was at night when radar gave us good warning and emergency turns by both convoys avoided a collision. But both occasions were highly hazardous, and on the second occasion there was a regrettable display of fireworks by escorts who should have known better, which illuminated both convoys for miles.

There was another aspect to icebergs which should not be forgotten. For some reason or other, an iceberg to the asdic operator seems to make the same noise as a submarine proceeding on the surface. Moreover, as its bulk is mainly below the surface, it sometimes presents only a small radar echo which might be mistaken for a submarine. The danger of this situation in a fog is only too clear, and one can picture the scene on the bridge of a rather green ship with a keen but ignorant team:

'Hydrophone effect bearing green thirty — classified submarine,' would come smartly from the asdic operator.

'Starboard twenty, full ahead both engines — stand by to ram,' would be the eager response of the Officer of the Watch.

And the Wumph! as the bows crumpled on the iceberg would be heard for miles!

THE CONVOY SYSTEM

I would like now to discuss the convoy system in which two main fallacies, which for years have confused thinking on this important subject, still exist, I fear, in circles which should know better. I refer to the widespread belief that the convoy system necessarily represents a 'defensive' strategy; and on the other, to the declaration of many seafaring men — who should also know better — that merchant seamen are not capable of sailing in convoy owing to the problems of discipline and station-keeping.

The short history of convoys which follows below will, I hope, dispose of both these fallacies without further argument.

There was a third great fallacy, which also still circulates, that convoys cause serious port congestion and slow up delivery rates of cargo. This fiction weighed heavily with the economists and politicians and was eagerly grasped by the naval opponents of the convoy system. However, it can be shown that, unless it is badly organized, a convoy system is less likely to cause port congestion than the random arrival of independent ships. In fact, it dovetails well with the port organization precisely because it plans and controls ship movements. Furthermore, because of the smaller loss rate to be expected, convoy delivery rates of shipping under attack have usually proved greater than those of independently sailed ships. It would take, however, too much space to give the statistics and proof here.

The English convoy system started around these islands in the early thirteenth century. When King John lost Normandy to Philip of France in 1204, the English trade-routes to

Bordeaux and Bayonne with cargoes of wine and woad became vulnerable to attack from the flank.

Even at this early time, therefore, ships were ordered to sail in groups with an armed escort, with satisfactory results. But in 1336 it was found that ship-owners were trying to dodge convoy and sail independently in order to get in ahead of their commercial rivals, and, as a result, the destruction of shipping became so serious that Edward III forbade ships to sail except in convoy.

Convoys assembled at Harwich and Portsmouth, and Surveyors, who were the equivalent of the modern Naval Control of Shipping Officers, were appointed to inspect convoys before sailing. The convoys varied between 100 and 200 sail; in 1372 fifteen ships and 'five barges furnished for war' were provided as escorts, and the owners of these armed merchantmen were compensated for their services out of a tax levied on the wine imported.

Each convoy was under the charge of two Royal Officers: the Commodore, whose duties correspond to those of the modern Commodore of Convoy, and the Escort Commander. The passage of these convoys was regarded as a naval operation.

With the introduction of gunpowder, convoy was still found to be the most effective way of protecting shipping. In the early sixteenth century, Spain had become a great sea power with a valuable trade with its colonial empire overseas. Privateers began to cause serious losses and, after trying without success a system of controlled independent sailings along patrolled routes, the Spaniards adopted the well-tried method of convoy. By 1550 the Spanish *flotas* plied regularly between Europe and the Spanish Main, escorted by fast, well-armed warships known as the Indian Guard. Year after year, privateers, both French and English, attempted to capture the treasure ships in these convoys, but they never succeeded. It is not generally known, for instance, that the Spanish Force which captured Sir Richard Grenville in the *Revenge* was the old-time equivalent of the modern support group!

About this time, in the 1580s, the English had some success in taking Portuguese caracks in the East Indian trade, but these ships were invariably sailing independently.

Both in the Anglo-Dutch wars and in the French wars of the seventeenth and eighteenth centuries, both sides sailed their merchant ships in escorted convoys, which were covered by the main fleet, and the prohibitive premiums placed by Lloyd's on ships sailing alone ensured that convoy was generally used.

In the Napoleonic wars convoy was obligatory for English ships, and Lloyd's would not insure vessels sailing independently except those licensed by the Admiralty to do so because they were exceptionally fast and well armed. The convoy system was very extensive and its organization thorough and complicated.

An extract from a directive for the protection and conduct of a fleet of merchant ships at sea, dated 1794, is of great interest:

> To take the requisite care of a large fleet of merchant vessels, there should be in the convoy a number of frigates, which are to be distributed ahead, astern and on the wings of the fleet, which is always to be kept in the order of three, four, five or six columns, according to the number it may be composed of. Some other frigates are also to be sent on the look-out, in order that the commanding officer may be informed of what passes at a certain distance, and warned in good time of the approach of the enemy.
>
> If the frigates which are sent to look-out should discover an enemy of superior force, they will make it known by signal, and perhaps it may be thought advisable that they should steer

a different course from that of the fleet, in order to deceive the hostile ships in sight.

The line of battleships are to hold themselves a little ahead and to windward of the weather column of the fleet; because, in that position, they will be able with promptitude to attend wherever their presence may be necessary. The commanding officer must not neglect to have all suspicious and neutral ships chased and even stopped by the frigates about him, and which are always to be supported by one or two lines of battleships, according to the exigency of the circumstances.

The degree of progress which the whole fleet will make will be regulated by that of the worst-going ships, which, however, are to be abandoned when found to cause too great a loss of time; for sometimes it is better to risk a small loss than to expose the whole by delay.

There will be placed between the columns, sloops of war and other swift-sailing vessels to maintain order and keep the ships in their stations. Their particular business will be to get the tardy ships to make more sail, and to oblige those which may be out of their post to resume it. In the evening they will give an account, to the frigates having charge of going the round, of those which have not well manoeuvred and these will be reported to the Commodore.

During the night the same order will be maintained, except with respect to the look-out frigates which are to be called in within a certain distance of the fleet, and which are to be allowed lights as well as the rest of the men-of-war. They are to be particularly careful to oblige all straggling ships to return to the convoy, and to fire, without hesitating, on all strange vessels coming from the main sea, in order to give the alarm. Every night they are to be supported on the wings by some line of battleships.

Some of these convoys contained several hundred sailing ships which travelled safely in company in all types of weather.

About 150 years later the Escort Commander of 1939 could have read these instructions with great profit; for, despite the experiences of 1917-18, there was no modern version available for him. Moreover, those employed in drafting such instructions in the Admiralty and at the various Command Headquarters could equally have profited from them.

By 1914 we had passed through virtually one hundred years of peace, during which the serious study of maritime war had been sadly neglected by naval officers — except for an American, Captain Mahan. The lessons of the past were forgotten and a host of new and quite unsound theories were evolved.

Until 1917, when the convoy system was forced on to a protesting Admiralty, all merchant ships sailed independently, with results only too well known. The U-boats, the twentieth-century equivalent of privateers, had, by the end of February 1917 when unrestricted warfare against shipping had been in force only a month, sunk 1,504 merchant ships, despite unremitting efforts to counter these attacks by numerous patrolling and hunting forces, both surface and air.

In addition to the fallacies mentioned previously, every sort of other reason was advanced in order to prove that convoys were impossible. The most unsound, perhaps, was that steamers would be unable to keep station or to manoeuvre in convoy, and apparently the vast armadas of sailing ships, which had manoeuvred safely and which provided a so much more difficult problem than in the days of steam, had been forgotten.

Lack of escorts was another reason which proved incorrect in practice, as also was the alleged difficulty of organizing the American end of homeward-bound Atlantic convoys. The success of the escorted sailings between Harwich and the

Hook of Holland, and of the escorted convoys carrying coal from South Wales to the French ports, were equally ignored. Lastly, it was contended that convoys would provide such an easy target — a forecast which proved completely wrong in practice, for the attacks were found more difficult, and moreover, the location of convoys proved a far more formidable task than that of finding independent shipping sailing along patrolled routes.

Another factor which hid the necessity for convoy was the fact that the Government War Risk Insurance Scheme, introduced at the beginning of the war, took away from Lloyd's their natural function of warning the Admiralty when sinkings were growing heavy and, as a corollary, when convoy was necessary. In the Napoleonic wars the pressure of the insurance market made certain that no ship sailed independently, otherwise they could not be insured; but between 1914 and 1917 the Government paid and no one cared. Also the statistics in the Admiralty of the volume of shipping sailing on the oceans were grossly inadequate, and the Admiralty, until 1917, were completely misinformed, by a factor of over ten, about the number of ships which would be required to sail in ocean convoy from these Islands each week, thus raising unfounded opposition to the introduction of convoys.

The introduction of the convoys in June 1917 had spectacular and immediate results. Wherever it was started, the volume of sinkings fell, and by the time the convoy system had been fully organized both on the oceans and in coastal waters, the U-boat war against shipping had been defeated — though U-boat mine-laying remained a serious problem until the Armistice. We had returned to the ancient system of waging maritime war, and success had been instantaneous.

In 1939 we find almost the same story, though, fortunately for the Allies, Lieutenant Lemp, in U-30, mistook the unarmed liner *Athenia* for a troopship during the night of 3rd/4th September, and sank her without warning. This ensured the introduction of the convoy system which up to then had only been intended to be started if the Germans adopted 'unrestricted' warfare against shipping.

Despite much doubt, convoy remained the core of our maritime strategy throughout the war, and despite many mistakes in the application of old-established principles of convoy protection, the results speak for themselves.

The tragic disaster of Convoy PQ 17 in 1942 provides only too clear an example, for while this convoy was kept together, its losses were negligible. Only after it had been instructed by the Admiralty to scatter owing to the threat of surface attack, were the individual ships destroyed, one by one, by U-boats and aircraft.

Up to 31st May 1943, when the Battle of the Atlantic had, in effect, been won, over two-thirds of all ships sunk by U-boats had been sunk when *not* in convoy; while the convoy escort or support forces — the so-called 'defensive' forces — sank two-thirds of all U-boats destroyed. The vast effort devoted up to the end of May 1943 to the 'offensive' methods — such as strategic bombing and mining, patrols by surface craft and aircraft, hunting groups, and transit area offensives — sank only one-third of the total of the U-boats destroyed. Indeed, up to May 1943 not one U-boat had been destroyed by strategic bombing of bases and building yards, and December 1944 was the best month of the war for production of U-boats, although by this time, bombing and mining were seriously interfering with the flow of U-boats to the operational area.

In other words, convoy is the essence of offence, for instead of dispersing your forces in search of an enemy whose object is to avoid them, it forces the enemy to scatter his forces in search of your shipping, and when he finds it either to fight on your own ground and on your own terms in order to reach your shipping, or to remain impotent. As Admiral Sims said in 1918, 'it is a purely offensive measure'.

On 7th December 1941, the U.S. Navy had forgotten his words. No plans existed for convoys on the east coast of America, and merchant ships sailed independently, with warships and aircraft 'patrolling the routes'. The results were disastrous. Shipping losses were critically high, and the U-boats were often able to pick off their victims by gunfire on the surface. Although small reinforcements of corvettes, trawlers and maritime aircraft were sent by the United Kingdom to help stop the slaughter of shipping at a time when we were very hard pressed in our own waters, it was only when the convoy system was instituted that losses diminished, and this occurred with almost magical effect in June and July 1942.

The opinion of the German High Command and of the U-boat Commanders was very clear. They did not want to attack convoys. It was too difficult and was only to be attempted if enough 'independents' could not be found. Contrary to the general impression, the ace U-boat Commanders such as Prien, Kretchmer, and Schepke gained most of their successes by sinking ships sailing singly and not by attacks on convoys. Indeed, these very three men were lost or captured in an attempt to attack the same convoy.

Not only did convoy provide protection against U-boats, but also against every other form of attack at sea. Against air attack, independent shipping was helpless, whereas a powerful antiaircraft escort, sometimes with fighters from escort carriers, could be provided for convoys. In surface raids independent ships were easy prey, and of the 800,000 tons of shipping sunk by surface raider, only five ships of 33,000 tons were sunk in escorted convoy.

The reason for this is clear. By attacking an escorted convoy the raider risks damage by the escort, usually in an area many hundreds of miles away from his base. In practice, surface raiders, whether warship or disguised merchantman, have always found that they cannot afford to take this risk. Thus, whether it was pocket battleships like the *Scheer*, battlecruisers like the *Scharnhorst* and *Gneisenau*, or heavy cruisers like the *Hipper*, the presence of a cruiser or even a destroyer escort was enough to prevent attack. On one escorted convoy only — and that with nothing but a single armed merchant cruiser as defence — did a serious attack develop in the last war, and, in this instance, as the glorious epic of the *Jervis Bay* recalls, the majority (thirty-two out of thirty-seven) of the convoy escaped.

It was the same story with mines, for here it was possible to escort convoys down channels especially swept for them, whereas independent ships were inclined to get out of the channel, which, also, could not be specially cleared for their passage.

Finally, many of the clashes between major units of the fleet took place either in the vicinity of a convoy or to cover or prevent its sailing, and again we find that the convoy system proved to be the base around which all our plans developed.

Perhaps the most dangerous and misleading phrases used in discussing maritime warfare are those of 'protection of shipping lanes' and the 'defence of our lines of communication'. Over the centuries it has been proved and re-proved that it is impossible to protect a 'sea lane' unless it is very narrow and very short. The aim is to protect ships, not bits of water — ships which are proceeding from one port to another. The only area of ocean in which we are really interested is the part in which the ship is physically placed at the time.

This proposition, expressed slightly differently, is a strong argument for the convoy system; and the phrase 'protection of shipping lanes' has been responsible for much senseless steaming by warships and many unnecessary losses of merchant ships.

Another dangerous concept, which was tied to 'defence of sea lanes', was the hunting or patrol group when applied to anti-submarine warfare.

In the early days of the last war, hunting groups of aircraft-carriers, cruisers and battlecruisers were formed to find and destroy the enemy surface warships which were still at large on the oceans. One of these groups was responsible for sinking the *Graf Spee*. But, unfortunately, the problem of finding battleships and submarines is totally different. The detection range of an asdic set was under a mile; while the range at which a battleship could be seen was up to fifteen miles, and more if aircraft were available. The chances of running down a U-boat in the vast expanses of the ocean were thus infinitesimal. But the lure of the words 'hunting group' was too much for us — to have groups of destroyers dashing about the ocean in search of their prey gave a tremendous impression of action, of the offensive spirit; while the dull, routine work of escorting convoys gave an impression of passive defence.

But the escort of convoys was the only effective way, both of protecting the merchant ships and of destroying the U-boats; while the aimless dashing about the ocean of the hunting or patrolling groups was a useless waste of valuable ships. Many thousands of miles were so wasted by destroyers in the first year of the war.

Support groups were a different concept altogether. As the name implied, they supported convoys which were being threatened or attacked, and they did little aimless patrolling. The description 'hunter-killer' group which the United States Navy used for the very successful groups of escort carriers and destroyers which it formed in 1942 has proved unfortunate. The successes gained were either when supporting convoys, or when — a very rare event in war — the position of the hunted U-boat was exactly known.

Even now, when I hear the term 'hunter-killer' used in peacetime exercises, I wonder if all is well with our policy!

It may well be asked, 'What of the future in a nuclear war?' Field-Marshal Montgomery has called attention in a public lecture to what he calls the 'increased importance of sea power' in the nuclear age. He predicts that in the nuclear era the passage of men and supplies over the sea will be more and not less important than ever before. The advent of the megaton and the kiloton bomb and of nuclear propulsion of submarines has certainly made a solution of the problems of defending convoys in a global nuclear war a more difficult task than ever before. Jet aircraft with long range have especially increased the difficulty.

Nevertheless, the problem should be considered in terms of convoy *warfare* rather than of convoy defence. It will then be appreciated that there may be compensating developments in the powers of defence that make attacking a convoy as daunting a task as ever in the past, though its size, shape and density may be very different to what we have been accustomed to. And can we be sure that a future conflict will include the use of nuclear weapons?

I believe firmly, therefore, although in no position to prove it with facts or figures, that the convoy system, modified and developed to counter the new weapons, will again solve the problem of shipping defence. For instance, by increasing the spacing of ships when nuclear attack from the air threatens, much of the danger will be dissipated. For this and other reasons inherent in the system, I believe that no effort should be spared to continue research into the past and thought into the future on this vital subject.

An island like ours must depend on the sea for its imports and its exports. Carriage by air cannot compete economically with bulk cargoes.

Let us hope and pray that we shall never again have to sustain this island in war, or its forces fighting overseas. But the possibility, especially of the second alternative, is always with us, and we must be prepared, both mentally and physically.

APPENDIX I: AUTHOR'S NAVAL BACKGROUND

IN May 1926, at the age of thirteen and a half, I went to the Royal Naval College, Dartmouth, as a Naval Cadet. In the last three terms cadets were taken for week-long cruises in the old coal-burning minesweeper *Forres*, where we did all the ship's duties, from stoking the boilers to navigation. Otherwise the training at Dartmouth was carried out either ashore at the College or in boats on the River Dart.

I was sent to Devonport in January 1930 to join my first ship, the *Renown*, Flagship of the Battlecruiser Squadron, and after eight months in her I was promoted to Midshipman, which resulted in a pay increase from four to five shillings a day. While in the ship, which formed part of the Home Fleet, we went on two Spring Cruises at the end of which came the Combined Fleet Exercises with the Mediterranean Fleet and fleet assemblies at Gibraltar and Palma. One saw a carrier or two, seven battleships, three battlecruisers, a dozen cruisers, fifty or sixty destroyers and two flotillas of submarines. It was a wonderful experience to watch the fleets manoeuvring.

In the early summer of 1931 I was appointed to the *Dragon*, an elderly cruiser on the West Indies station. Six of us midshipmen took passage to Bermuda in the liner *Orduna* and this proved an interesting introduction to Merchant Service life.

Our time in the *Dragon* was a very happy one. Although there was little fleet work, the long independent cruises around America and the West Indies gave an opportunity for members of the gunroom to be given jobs carrying more responsibility than midshipmen had in a big fleet.

In the autumn of 1932 the ship came home to pay off at Chatham. It had been a good commission and one of the most interesting times was, of course, in September 1931, when the Atlantic Fleet mutinied at Invergordon. The *Dragon* was then on the west coast of the United States, and life on board continued undisturbed. None of us could understand what was going on at home and relationships between officers and men were unimpaired.

Four of us in the gunroom were due to take our seamanship examination before the end of the year. Accordingly we were appointed to the battleship *Rodney* to finish our last three months as midshipmen, and although we did not like the idea, we were fortunate, for we were given few ship's duties and were allowed to concentrate on preparations for our seamanship exam which was rightly regarded as a most important hurdle in one's early career — without it promotion to Sub-Lieutenant was impossible. We got plenty of sea time in the *Rodney* and much valuable experience was gained. The results of the exam were most satisfactory, for I got my first-class certificate.

The three years at sea as a cadet and midshipman had been interesting, varied and useful and I enjoyed every minute, but there were two deficiencies. I had not been on the Junior Officers' Air Course in an aircraft-carrier, and I had not done any destroyer time, both of which should have formed part of a midshipman's career.

Ever since standing on the quarterdeck of the *Renown* one lovely evening in the Mediterranean and watching the six flotillas of the Combined Fleets manoeuvring together in close order, I had made up my mind that I must get into destroyers.

There were nine ships in each flotilla and the sight was unforgettable. The ships of the Mediterranean Fleet with their light-grey paint and gleaming brightwork were especially memorable.

In those days, to get into destroyers meant that one started as the Sub, then became the Number Two (or navigator) and after one job as First Lieutenant, hoped to get a Command. But it was to take much time and trouble and I never did achieve each rung of the ladder.

After some fifteen months spent doing courses at the Royal Naval College, Greenwich, and at various technical schools at Portsmouth, I successfully completed all the required courses for Sub-Lieutenant. During the eight months at Greenwich, I joined the Naval Flying Club and, with the aid of its subsidy, learnt to fly a Moth aircraft at the London Flying Club at Hanworth. Aviation was obviously of very great importance to the navy and I wanted to find out if I had any gifts in the air! I went solo and got my A licence, achieving some forty or fifty hours flying; but I was not a good pilot and I discarded any plans to apply for the Fleet Air Arm, and put my name down for a destroyer and the first job as a Sub.

However, in April 1934, I was appointed to the Royal Yacht *Victoria and Albert* for the summer season. It was a wonderful experience, but the seagoing was confined to engine trials in May off the south coast and the trip from Portsmouth to Cowes and back in August!

After Cowes Week two of us Subs managed to get leave to do the Junior Officers' Air Course, which we had missed as midshipmen and which was intended to give all officers a good appreciation of the problems of the Fleet Air Arm. We spent an interesting six weeks in the *Courageous* and I got a lot of flying in the back seats of Baffins and Seals. The Torpedo

Officer, who had been my divisional officer in the *Renown*, had an exceptionally able brain and was investigating some new ideas in torpedo attacks from aircraft. I spent much time photographing the tracks of the torpedoes from a Seal which was circling overhead and then analysing the results. It proved unfortunate that the Torpedo Officer's ideas of making the torpedoes glide by fitting them with wings were not well received. He was later shown to be correct.

But my time in the *Courageous* was valuable and gave an introduction to problems of the air and also to the R.A.F. officers who then piloted some of the aircraft.

Then, instead of the destroyer for which I had hoped, I was appointed to the *Durban*, Flagship of the 3rd Cruiser Squadron in the Mediterranean. In October 1934 I took passage to Malta in the cruiser *Berwick* which was on its way to the Far East. I remember vividly my first watch on the bridge. Although now a Lieutenant, with a watchkeeping certificate, I had, in fact, never kept a watch alone and the certificate obtained in the Royal Yacht was rather a fraud! However, I avoided trouble and gained confidence.

After joining the *Durban* I became one of the watch-keeping divisional officers and later, when a new cruiser, the *Arethusa*, took the flag, also the ship's Signal Officer.

During the *Durban*'s commission in the Mediterranean the fleet was kept busy, for the Abyssinian War, the Spanish Civil War and the Arab Rebellion in Palestine all affected the navy. We spent most of the time at Haifa which became a 3rd Cruiser Squadron base, and this resulted in my getting a spell of active service ashore. The army were very short of artillery and the *Durban* hoisted out one of the two-pounder Pom Poms and mounted it on a lorry which we hired in Haifa. I was put in charge of the crew of four sailor volunteers and we had a most pleasant break from life on board. The rebellion had dislocated the economy, many roads were impassable without an armed escort and we were used to protect convoys of trucks on the main roads, assisted by armoured cars and a lorry fitted with a searchlight. Our beat was the Tulkharn-Jenin-Nablus triangle and we went out most nights and rested by day. I had a good gun's crew, the gun fired many hundreds of rounds without a stoppage and we got on very well with the soldiers.

After some weeks I was relieved by another officer from the ship, but soon after rejoining the *Durban* I took a mixed platoon of seamen and stokers ashore to help the police with the control of the Souk at Haifa. We had a busy two weeks ashore, though we did more firefighting than street-fighting, and my main problem was to prevent accidents due to the careless handling of the platoon's weapons! We were effective, however, and this was due to the cheerful manners of the sailors, who soon made friends with the Arabs, rather than to our martial efficiency.

In the autumn of 1936 the ship went home to pay off into reserve and to my horror I was appointed to a short physical-training course before being sent as Seamanship and Sports Officer to H.M.S. *Impregnable*, the boys' training establishment at Devonport. I had only myself to blame! During my time in the *Durban* all junior officers were invited to state their preferences for specialization. I was still determined not to specialize and to get into destroyers, but I was very vulnerable, having got a full house of firsts in my Sub's courses and might easily have got conscripted by one of the schools. So I put down 'General Service' (which meant destroyers), Staff Duties, and Physical Training as my three preferences, secure in the thought that one could not get selected for a staff course until much more senior and that as I was the least 'gymnastic' officer in the navy, I would never get chosen for P.T.! All was not lost, however, since the short course did not qualify as a specialization.

After a strenuous year in the *Impregnable*, I was transferred to the Royal Naval College, Dartmouth, as a house officer and spent a pleasant spell of some two years there until the outbreak of war. I was still hankering after destroyers and during both my summer leaves I had managed to get myself appointed 'additional' to one of the Home Fleet ships — to the *Foresight* in 1938, and to the *Ashanti* in 1939. These spells were good value, for the ships were extremely busy with fleet exercises and welcomed an extra hand on board. The Captains were both kind and patient and taught me a lot. In addition, during the Munich crisis of 1938, I was sent to the *Vanquisher* which was lying at the Nore, but we had time only to reach Beachy Head on our way to Portland when the 'war' was called off and I went back to Dartmouth.

In the Easter leave of 1939 I did a week's anti-submarine course at the A/S school at Portland, H.M.S. *Osprey*. I must confess that the main reason for this keenness was because I wanted to ride in the Cattistock and Blackmore Vale Point-to-Points, and the *Osprey* provided free accommodation! But I did get to sea in ships of the local flotilla and learnt a bit about A/S.

So when the war came, despite three years on the beach, I had some destroyer experience behind me, and already knew that no other career in the world could have provided such an interesting, happy and satisfying life as the navy.

APPENDIX II: NAMES OF B 7 ESCORT GROUP COMMANDING OFFICERS

Name: Lt.-Com. R. E. Sherwood, R.N.R., now Captain, D.S.O., *Ship*: *Tay*, *Battles at which present*: HX 231, ONS 5, SC 130.

Name: Lt. R. Hart, R.N., now Captain, D.S.O., D.S.C., *Ship*: *Vidette*, *Battles at which present*: HX 231, ONS 5, SC 130, supporting.

Name: Lt.-Com. J. Plomer, R.C.N.V.R., now Commodore, R.C.N., D.S.C., *Ship*: *Sunflower*, *Battles at which present*: ONS 5, SC 130, supporting.

Name: Lt.-Com. M. G. Rose, R.A.N.V.R., now Captain, *Ship*: *Alisma*, *Battles at which present*: HX 231.

Name: Captain Lt. R. Atkinson, R.N.R., now Lt.-Com., D.S.C., *Ship*: *Pink*, *Battles at which present*: HX 231, ONS 5, SC 130, supporting.

Name: Lt. Chesterman, R.N.R., now Captain, D.S.C., *Ship*: *Snowflake*, *Battles at which present*: HX 231, ONS 5, SC 130.

Name: Lt. H. A. Stonehouse, R.N.R., now Captain, D.S.C., *Ship*: *Loosestrife*, *Battles at which present*: HX 231[6], ONS 5, SC 130, supporting.

---

[6] The ship took part in HX 231, but not Stonehouse.

ACKNOWLEDGEMENTS

The author acknowledges with thanks permission granted to quote extracts from the following:

The War at Sea, Vol. 2, by Captain S. W. Roskill (H.M.S.O.)

Ten Years and Twenty Days by Admiral Doenitz (Weidenfeld & Nicholson)

He also acknowledges the following, which have been helpful:

The Fiercest Battle by Ronald Seth (Hutchinsons)

The War at Sea, Vol. 1, by Captain S. W. Roskill (H.M.S.O.)

The Battle of the Atlantic by Captain D. McIntyre (Batsford)

Narvik by Captain D. McIntyre (Evans)

Red Ensign by Owen Rutter (Robert Hale)

History of U.S. Naval Operations in World War Two by Samuel Eliot Morison (Little & Brown)

The Two Ocean War by S. E. Morison (Little & Brown)

U-boats at War by Harald Busch (Putnams)

The Hunters and the Hunted by Jochen Brennecks (Burke)

The last chapter has been based on papers written by Lt.-Comdr. D. W. Waters, R.N. retd., then in the Admiralty Historical Section and now at the National Maritime Museum, Greenwich, and by his colleague, the late Lt.-Comdr. D. Barley.

A NOTE TO THE READER

If you have enjoyed this book enough to leave a review on **Amazon** and **Goodreads**, then we would be truly grateful.
The Estate of Sir Peter Gretton

Sapere Books is an exciting new publisher of brilliant fiction and popular history.

To find out more about our latest releases and our monthly bargain books visit our website:
saperebooks.com

Printed in Great Britain
by Amazon

29859072R00141